Body of Knowledge

SUNY Series in Transpersonal and Humanistic Psychology

Richard D. Mann, Editor

Body of Knowledge

An Introduction
to Body/Mind Psychology

Robert Marrone

State University of New York Press

Published by
State University of New York Press, Albany

For information, address State University of New York
Press, State University Plaza, Albany, N.Y., 12246

Library of Congress Cataloging-in-Publication Data

    Marrone, Robert L.
      Body of knowledge: an introduction to body/mind psychology/
    Robert Marrone.
      p.   cm. — (SUNY series in transpersonal and humanistic
    psychology)
      Includes bibliographical references.
      ISBN 0-7914-0387-4. — ISBN 0-7914-0388-2 (pbk.)
      1. Mind and body. I. Title. II. Series.
    BF161.M365   1990
    150.19′8 — dc20

10 9 8 7 6 5 4 3 2

To Robert Hall, M.D.,
whose depth of compassion and breadth of knowledge
has touched the lives of so many, in so many ways.

Contents

Acknowledgments

Thanks, to my best friend and soul mate, Elayne Marie Azevedo, for continually showing me what it means to love and be loved; to my son, Jason, for always reminding me to kindle curiosity towards life; to my parents and family for their unswerving support through the many ping-pong games I've played in this life; and to good friends, old and new, who have encouraged me, including Steve Holsapple, Dee Eggleston, Tri Thong Dang and Pauline Haynes.

Thanks, to graduate student friends who have contributed greatly to this work, especially Dennis Norris and Gene Sweaney; and to colleagues who have encouraged my changes, as well as my work over the years, especially Professor Emeritus, David Lucas. And to others who have helped me track down hard to find material or offered heart-felt advice, including Professors Bruce Behrman, Arnold Golub, Joseph Heller, Lawrence Meyers, William Westbrook and Librarian, Stan Frost — all of California State University, Sacramento.

Thanks, to the many teachers and guides I have come to know over the years — and who have provided so much needed perspective and wisdom, including Dr. Victor Lovell of Prometheus Center in Palo Alto; Alyssa Hall, Michael Smith, Andrew Leeds and Richard Strozzi-Heckler of the Lomi School; the late Chogyam Trungpa, Rinpoche, of Naropa University in Boulder, Colorado; Dr. Martin Rogers of California State University, Sacramento for supervising my clinical training; and, to the late Dr. Alan Watts for encouraging me to "chase after the synthesis until it catches you."

Introduction

There is a time for keeping still and there is a manner of keeping still
which relates to every experience involving movement, whether the
movement is physical, mental, or spiritual.

—I Ching

Movement and stillness, expansion and contraction, as they manifest all around us, offer a glimpse, perhaps, into the heart of the matter. Consider, that before we experience a single sensation, emotion or
thought—even before we take our next breath, there is both movement
and stillness at the core of who we are. And even when the mind comes
to rest and the breath is soft and still, what is still going on?

It is the beating of our hearts.

Movement and stillness.

With each passing moment, it beats in our chest, twisting, expanding, contracting, over and over, one-hundred thousand times each
day — three billion beats in an average lifetime.[1]

It is a muscle — not a concept. We do not create it.

We do not beat our hearts.

Please pause for a moment now — and focus your awareness on
the sensations emanating from the middle of your chest.

Can you feel your heart beat?

Can you hear it? Is it soft and rhythmical?

Are you breathing in tune with its beat?

As you exhale, can you feel your heart relax?

Are you unclutching your heart now?

To answer such questions, we must first bring our awareness to
the body/mind experience of who we are — *now* — in this very moment. Our thoughts and concepts may come and go, memories may
fade, and our images of who we think we are may rise and burst like
bubbles on a lake. But the body is always with us because, fundamentally, we are body, we act through body, and we perceive the world and
each other through bodies. We are *lived-body*,[2] and our experience of
being-in-the-world is created and given form through our bodies.

It is from a murky, undifferentiated state of pure embodiment —
of body/mind unity — that we first act upon the surrounding world
and, in so doing, experience ourselves as different from it.

Observe the newborn infant or toddler exploring the world. The child's initial sense of unity with its surroundings is repeatedly ruptured in its interaction with those surroundings. Consider little Jennifer, as the infant's pleasure-seeking lips search for mother's nipple, the simple imperative takes form ... *"mommy not I."* In the collision between baby and coffee table, the statement is uttered once again ... *"coffee table not I."* And, too, as a toddler, drawn in fascination to the movement of sticky fingers, Jennifer touches each one accompanied by the statement, *"my finger, my finger."* And so on, by way of these experiences of lived-body, our *sense-of-self* or "I-ness" begins its seemingly endless process of delineation and affirmation.

To experience *embodiment* is to experience being, thoroughly, "in the lived-body" — from moment-to-moment — sensing precisely those body-sensations, feelings, and thoughts which give form to our sense-of-self.

And yet, consider the *body* described in textbooks and encyclopedias. They are composed almost exclusively of descriptions of structures and functions; with elaborate illustrations of neurons, organ systems, and such. They present us with information about a *concept of body*, but say virtually nothing about the experience of lived-body.

The same may be said of modern psychology. Here too, with noted exceptions, it is assumed that we experience our bodies in the same way a disinterested observer notices, say, a bus, a flower, or any other "thing" in the surrounding environment. For instance, in James V. McConnell's[3] introductory psychology textbook, now in its fifth edition and one of the best-selling books of its kind, he states, that " ... with minor exceptions, the physical changes that occur in your body are *pretty much the same* no matter what type of emotional upheaval you are undergoing." He says that the body doesn't determine our emotional reaction to a situation, instead it is " ... how you *perceive* and *feel* about a situation that determines your bodily reaction rather than vice versa." However, the question of who it is doing the feeling and perceiving, if not an embodied being, is never addressed— although a disembodied mind is highly suspect.

From theories of personality to theories of psychopathology, present day psychology begins with the concept of body and then proceeds to appliqué it with personal meanings which are thought to produce a body-concept or body image.

So too, in our most cherished beliefs about medicine, psychotherapy, healing, and personal growth, the body and mind are arbitrarily split and isolated. There are doctors to heal the body and *other* doctors to heal the mind. In the practice of psychotherapy, for instance, the therapist sits and verbally explores the client's personal history and emotional issues with words, alone. All can agree, however, that our histories and issues as self-reflecting beings are buried, not exclusively in mind and its often dim remembrances, but in the sensations, the feelings, and the bodily movements which give form to our experience in the first place.

The most fundamental source of our own body-of-knowledge, the lived-body experience, has been virtually excluded from our cultural body-of-knowledge. And yet, after more than three centuries, a force is emerging from within modern psychology which is questioning the old assumption of a split between body and mind. To these body/mind researchers and theorists, the lived-body is not a severed head studying a mirror-reflection of the rest of itself. The dualistic assumption of separate body and mind is, instead, wedded to an alternative assumption — an assumption of body/mind unity, as well as acknowledgment that my lived-body, and your lived-body set the ground rules for all that issues from them, including the concept of "mind."

This book is my attempt to share with you what I am learning about Body/Mind Psychology: its roots, its theories, and its approaches; and to survey with you the paths being settled by this emerging force — in *healing*, *communication*, and *conscious living*.

It is also a book about living our lives in a disembodied, impersonal world of images and concepts — or, alternatively, living our lives in a world made saner and more meaningful by virtue of our complete, embodied participation in the world.

Part one of this work, Groundwork, explores the historical roots and theoretical underpinnings of this emerging force in psychology. Beginning with Sigmund Freud, and then to his student Wilhelm Reich — the theoretical and practical bases for a Body/Mind Psychology were laid. Now, they continue in the work of numerous contemporary researchers, theorists and healers.

In part two, Framework, I review the design features of a working body/mind bridge, under construction, and consider some of the breakthroughs in psychosomatic medicine, physiological psychology, holography, quantum physics, and clinical research which are giving form to new methodologies and healing models.

In part three, Bodywork, I review the ways in which this new body/mind paradigm is being applied in clinical research and in the practice of psychotherapy. I offer a body reading, followed by case profiles and session notes of body/mind psychotherapy drawn from a wide array of therapists, counselors, and other healers.

Finally, in part four, Wonderwork, I suggest some of the new vistas opening up to us in our understanding of personal healing, cultural renewal, and spiritual awakening as we prepare for entry into a new millennia.

Personal Introduction

My training and practice in the field of psychology has often felt like a sort of ping-pong game—with exclusive study of the body at one end of the table, and the exclusive study of the mind at the other end.

Much of my graduate training involved experimental and physiological psychology—and research with animals, including fish, mice, rats, cats, monkeys, and dolphins. I've treated Siamese fighting fish with various drugs in attempts to influence the intensity of their aggression. With colleagues, I've implanted brain electrodes, in rats and cats, in search of hypothalamic pleasure centers. I've taught dolphins to make color and shape discriminations, and have spent long hours observing Rhesus monkeys as they interacted with infant offspring.

My postdoctoral position brought me to the other side of the table — to one of the largest psychiatric facilities in the nation — where I conducted research on the effects of anti-psychotic and anti-anxiety agents on a population of outpatients. In this context, I became fascinated with the interior world of mind—and began to deeply question the paths I'd chosen in the field of psychology.

Two years later, having accepted a teaching position at California State University, I seemed to begin anew — this time with an ever-intensifying interest in clinical psychology. My clinical training extended over the next decade and involved study in the areas of Gestalt psychotherapy, psychoanalysis, psychodrama, and cognitive therapy.

The experience of sitting in my office each day, conducting the "talking cure," was, for me, analogous to having thoroughly explored one land mass only to be parachuted into another. From neurons, synapses and brain homogenates, I was now discussing the deepest of life's issues with my clients in terms of problem solving strategies, emotional catharsis, and archetypal dreams. My curiosity had led me to a newer vista. What was so sorely missing, however, was a bridge; some connection which would allow me to make sense of what I had learned about the physical body—and was discovering, on a daily basis, about the human mind.

About mid-way through my clinical training, I was introduced to the body work technique of postural realignment, called Rolfing. I attended a university presentation by Bob Prichard,[4] a Rolfing practitioner, which I viewed with great skepticism. He explained that with deep pressure applied to the muscles and fascia, the body could be straightened and placed in alignment with gravity. This, he went on to explain, would relieve stress, back pain and create increased bodily movement and fluidity, which had profound effects on the personality.

On the recommendation of a colleague, Charles Tart,[5] who had recently completed ten sessions of Rolfing, I decided to be Rolfed myself.

With each session, as Prichard's thumbs, fists, and elbows stretched muscles and tendons in my body, powerful memories and emotions would push through and take over my consciousness. As he pushed against the muscles of my chest and diaphragm, I began to weep uncontrollably. As he worked at loosening the muscles of my shoulders and upper back, I went into a rage—flooded with childhood memories and resentments which had been buried deep within.

These experiences made clear to me that my deepest memories and emotions were not locked, exclusively, in memory engrams somewhere in my head. Rather, I had learned that deep stimulation of the muscles and viscera of my body could release memories and feelings into my conscious awareness — without my conscious intention of doing so.

I was truly baffled! Very little of my training in physiological psychology had ever hinted at this kind of connection between body and mind. My training in clinical psychology, although it offered more in the way of theories of body image and body concept, was just as securely built on what I was coming to view as a spurious assumption— namely, that body and mind are separate and distinct realms of existence and study.

Where? I began to wonder, does the mind begin and the body end —and the mind end and the body begin? And furthermore, I wondered, what would exploring such questions suggest to the theory and practice of psychotherapy and self-healing?

In 1977, I was invited to teach a course in States of Consciousness at Naropa University, a Buddhist university in Boulder, Colorado. On my way to class one morning, I was drawn to the sounds coming from a nearby classroom. As I peeked in, I saw the instructor demonstrating an approach to psychotherapy which involves both the mind and body. I watched as he applied deep pressure to the chest muscles of his student volunteer. As he pressed more deeply, the student's hands folded into fists, his jaw tightened and he began to pound the massage table, screaming "no, never, no," over and over again.

The instructor asked, "Who are you speaking to now?"

The student yelled, angrily, "My goddamn father!"

Maintaining pressure on the pectoralis muscles with his thumbs, the instructor replied, "Tell him everything you want to tell him now."

The young man began to pound the table with renewed force, saying, "Why did you do this to me? Why couldn't you just love me or hold me? Why did you beat me, and mom, why couldn't you just love us, why?" At this point, the student's body softened as he began to weep uncontrollably. The instructor gently pulled the young man's arms so that he assumed a partial sitting position, placed his arms around him, pulled him tightly to his chest and began rocking him gently, back and forth, while the tears continued to stream down his face. I stood motionless, struck with awe at what I was witnessing.

The instructor was Robert Hall, co-founder of the Lomi School of psychotherapy. In the years to come, I would study with him, Richard Strozzi-Heckler, Alyssa Hall, and other founders of this particular approach; as well as the work of others on the vanguard of this body/mind approach to psychotherapy and self-healing.

I hope this little book, like a slim beam of laser, casts some of the light being generated by these exciting breakthroughs in humanistic/transpersonal psychology.

Notes

1. John, Da Free. You Do Not Beat Your Heart, *Laughing Man*, 1983, 4 (2), 56–63.

2. Valle, Ronald S. and Mark King, *Existential-Phenomenological Alternatives for Psychology*, 1978, Oxford University Press, New York.

3. McConnell, James V., *Understanding Human Behavior*, 1986, Holt, Rinehart and Winston, New York, p. 306.

4. Prichard, Robert. Structural Integration, In *Rediscovery of the Body: A Psychosomatic View of Life and Death*, Charles Garfield, ed., 1977, Dell Publishing, New York.

5. Tart, Charles. *States of Consciousness*, 1975, E. P. Dutton, New York.

Suggested Readings

Fisher, Seymour. *Body Consciousness*, 1973, Prentice Hall, Englewood Cliffs, New Jersey.

Lowen, Alexander. *The Betrayal of the Body*, 1969, Macmillan, New York.

Schilder, Paul. *The Image and Appearance of the Human Body*, 1950, International Universities Press, New York.

Part One
Groundwork

1

Bodies of Knowledge

> We have almost lost contact with the part of ourselves which resonates
> with other animals and with Nature. It is that part of ourselves that en-
> ables us to experience the spiritual unity of our own being with all
> beings and to know intuitively that we and all life are of the same origin
> and Creation.[1]
>
> —Michael W. Fox, *Meditations with Animals*

Historical records inform us that each and every culture is composed of a body-of-knowledge which, instead of being a massive collection of information, is actually a superstructure of attitudes, beliefs,
and conditioned responses which sets the limits on what a society can
know. Within the framework of such a superstructure, a culture proceeds to establish its own "sense-of-itself."

In surveying the history of Western culture, historian P. A.
Sorokin[2] isolated three separate and unique bodies-of-knowledge,
each of which is structured upon and focused through a specific organ
of the human body: these organs are the heart, the head and the eye.

Heart Knowledge

Historical accounts reveal that our earliest ancestors inhabited a
heartfelt world in which they were immersed in the raw experience
provided by the structure and feel of the body itself. Sorokin terms this
heart knowledge, and speaks of it as knowledge grounded in the experience of lived-body.

Anthropologist Olivia Vlahos[3] also traces the beginnings of heart
knowledge to the experience of lived-body. Dimensions of the human
body, she points out, gave us our first measurements of space (twelve
inches = one foot), just as the movements of body provided our first
knowledge of seasonal rhythms and planetary cycles. Body fluids provided our first color meanings. To the Native American, for instance,
black fluid is the presence of all colors — and the crows are the spirit

presence of death in all things. Night is the color of the crow. Blue fluid is the color of sky and mother earth's nourishing lakes, rivers and rain. White fluid is the absence of color — the color beyond color. Like the white crane standing on one leg, white symbolizes the unhurried participant in the river of time — the divine wisdom.[4]

It was the structure and feel of the body which supplied our ancestors with the beginnings of human language, as well as our fundamental sense of a spiritual connectedness to all of the natural world.

In Julian Jaynes[5] historical analysis of the *Iliad*, the 24-volume epic poem describing many of the myths and tales of ancient Greece, numerous observations reveal a language not yet split into an inner-outer, mind-body separation. In fact, there appears to be an absence of words in the *Iliad* for either "mind" or "body" as separate entities. The word *soma*, which we currently use to mean "body," actually refers to a corpse or dead limbs in the *Iliad* — while the word *psyche*, with which we now refer to "mind," then referred to life-giving substances, such as blood or breath. In the *Iliad*, a dying warrior bleeds out his *psyche* onto the ground.

Head Knowledge

Historically, it was during the later Greek epoch, that evolutionary focus began to shift from the heart to the head — giving birth to the concept of "mind." During this period, the Greeks, and then the Romans, began to abstract their experience in earnest — learning not only to isolate, name and classify things, but also qualities, perceptions, feelings and actions. For each thought, there was a corresponding fact; for each word, a corresponding action, feeling, or thing. Through logical, rational thinking, linear excursions could now be launched into an apparent mini-universe which seemed to reside, primarily, in one's head.

In time, "mind" would be all but severed from the lived-body as it came under control of those who purported to understand its mysteries. Through shamanism, totemism and the rudiments of religious thinking, what was an ever-present spiritual connectedness to the natural world — would be packaged into separate languages, marketed by separate organizations, headed by separate individuals — each with his own indelible book-of-beliefs. By the time of the Medieval period, spiritual entities and gods were established who were seen as intermediaries between the lowly world of lived-body and the spiritual world "out there."

The original interconnected triad of God, Nature and Humanity was now fragmented into a hierarchical chain of command with God, the ruler of Nature and Humanity on top; and Humankind, born in the image of God, as ruler over Nature.

The scales had completely tipped, so that the immediate experience of unity and connectedness came to be abstracted, conceptualized and fantasized as crooked-nosed, goat-footed satyrs, one-footed giants, demons, dragons in the seas, and unicorns shuckin' trees.

If these demon-spirits and wrathful gods, along with their local representatives, were honored and obeyed, then any fear of the world out there would be lessened as the world came to appear more predictable, more easily controlled. And so, the experience of lived-body, which like a breath of fresh air, belonged to everyone — became controlled and, finally, dispensed by an elite caste of shamans, priests and head masters. Through their prayers and invocations to the spirit world, they promised, they would calm the fears embodied within all true believers.

> ... the body is the dark prison, the living death, the sense-endowed corpse, the grave thou bearest about with thee, the grave thou carriest around with thee, the thievish companion who hateth thee in loving thee, and envieth thee in hating thee.
>
> from a Christian Gnostic text

Rational thinking, as segregator and interpreter, reached its zenith in the seventeenth century, with the philosophical works of those we now refer to as the *Rationalists:* Spinoza, Descartes, Leibnitz, Locke, Pascal, and others. But it is Rene Descartes,[6] the French philosopher, who so completely epitomizes the Western rationalist by his successful attempt to thoroughly formalize the assumption of a body-mind split into the Western belief system — in what we now term *Cartesian dualism.*

In the midst of this changing world-view, Descartes recast the Medieval model with God at the apex and nature and humanity below. Any relationship between Humanity and Nature, claimed Descartes, is by way of divine revelation. Bishop Berkeley took the Humanity-Nature split one step further with his theory that human ideas were merely partial revelations of the divine mind.

However, it was left to Descartes to concretize the duality. In fact, there are few persons in Western history so associated with the devaluation of the body and overvaluation of the rational, logical, thinking mind.

Beginning with his first work, *Rules for the Direction of Mind* (1628), and culminating in his famous proposition, *I think, therefore I am*, Descartes firmly established the belief that, as beings, we cannot exist without *thinking* that we exist. The heart transplant was growing near to completion.

Eye Knowledge

Head-knowledge, founded on Greek logic, Medieval devaluation of the body, and the philosophical assumptions of the European Rationalists—was soon coupled to empiricism—an approach to knowledge which is more current and which centers knowledge in the human eye. To the empiricists, if it is real, it can be perceived and measured—and if it is not accessible to measurement, it is not a part of "reality."

The marriage of eye-knowledge to head-knowledge set the foundations for a scientific world-view which would, in short order, enrapture the Western mind. Sorokin informs us that *empiricism* gained tremendous ground very quickly because it so well supplied the Rationalists with laboratory measurement and statistical verification of what were, previously, merely armchair speculations and fantasies. Renaissance scientists could now replace the fiery fantasies of Medieval Christianity with a more positive set of abstractions.

In an evolutionary instant, Renaissance artists gained new perspective by applying mathematics to their works; new schools of biology arose; while Copernicus and Kepler devised radical theories which put the sun at the center of the universe. All in all, the limits on human knowledge were increasingly drawn by scientific principles, while heart-knowledge was increasingly exiled to another, more mysterious realm of existence.

As the scientific world-view gained increasing numbers of adherents, the body and mind came to be assumed as separate parts in an immense machine—one whose every component could be segregated, measured and verified. That the entire machine functioned according to strict scientific laws and principles, was rarely questioned — assured by new head masters.

The ghosts in the machine, such as human feelings, dreams, free will and consciousness, were now to be openly excluded from the body-of-knowledge by scientists wielding dual-edged swords: logical-illogical, rational-irrational, perception-misperception, and so on. The heart was now completely removed from the dominant body-of-knowledge—and even those thinkers who offered heartfelt speculations and theories, such as Sigmund Freud, would concede that their "soft" theories were merely stopgap measures until "hard" scientific evidence could be assembled.

Over time, the scientific world-view would be applied to the study of the universe, human cultures, behavior and the reconstruction of an entire civilization's body-of-knowledge.

Cranial Life

The language of the heart cries out to be heard. We ignore it at our peril.

James J. Lynch[7]

From the perspective of the comparative psychologist, D. O. Hebb[8] notes that in exploring the behavior of other animals, from ameba to primate, they get smarter, so to speak, more intelligent, more emotional and more intuitive. Chimpanzees are more emotional and brighter than reptiles; and human beings, up until the age of five years or so, are brighter and more emotional than chimpanzees. But adult humans, although they are intellectually brighter than children, do not seem to be more emotional or intuitional. Why? Hebb wonders. What happens to our capacity for being in touch with our emotional and intuitional ways of knowing? Why is heart knowledge all but absent from our dominant body-of-knowledge?

His answer is that as we mature in this culture, we learn to create a cocoon for ourselves to protect us from the unceasing bombardment of stimulation which we cannot, or will not, acknowledge and assimilate into our sense-of-self.

The creation of culture provides a protective capsule of set beliefs which serve to armor us against experiences which are upsetting or not easily denied or repressed. By devaluing lived-body; our feelings, emotions and intuitions, we attempt to protect ourselves from this central conflict and the primal experience of fear.

Like wearing a pair of gridded goggles, we cut, slice and abstract our primary experience of lived-body so as to create a secondary, conceptual order to our experiences which might lend itself to more predictability and control. To create this abstraction of experience, we have to split the heart world from the world of abstracted mind.

Pain, suffering and illness have been with humankind since the dawn of time. Causes and cures have ranged from homage to a galaxy of Gods and Goddesses; to dark and evil spirits; to wars on cancer, AIDS and drug abuse. But, through all of our modern attempts at healing ourselves, we have assumed the body and mind to be separate and distinct from each other. In a real sense, we have usually begun our search for solutions to life's issues of illness and health, madness and sanity, violence and peace, from within a body-of-knowledge which was, itself, ripped in two. Is it any wonder that our solutions have themselves been fragmented and incomplete.

In the process, we have been woefully slow to learn that purely objective-instrumental knowledge becomes destructive when it is heartless and used solely to gain power and control over Nature, the animal kingdom, and the human creative process. Today, this misuse of power has reached an apex, or abyss, where our primary motivations and goals take form, almost exclusively, as the desire for bigger profits, more information, greater prediction and control, and military superiority over wayward colonies and "evil empires."

Our connectedness to the whole, indeed, the holiness with which we once merged with all of Nature is now fractured and disturbed, and the sacred harmony is defiled and devalued. This is the heartbroken *ethos* of a technocratic, self-centered world-view that is turning the global landscape into a toxic wasteland — and is also responsible for the holocaust of the animal kingdom, as well as the human suffering wrought by famine, stress, cancer, birth defects and wars over depleting planetary resources.

Change of Heart

The concept of body/mind as an integrated, holistic system is actually quite new. However, the idea that each of us is inextricably linked to each other in a natural world is as old as humankind itself. From the perspective of a Body/Mind Psychology, we are in the process of drastically expanding the boundaries of an old fragmented body-of-knowledge into an integrated, lived-body-of-knowledge; one which values the human capacity for intuition, emotion and sense of connectedness, as much as our capacities to reason, predict and control.

The shift in consciousness involves not merely a change in opinions, values and beliefs, but, taken together, entails a change of heart, a revisioning of the very ground-of-meaning upon which each of us establishes our sense of self.

Theorist Willis Harman[9] argues that society is now moving from the Age of Science to the New Age of Consciousness. The old world-view, that gave legitimacy only to what science could observe, measure and explain, is shifting to a new world-view which acknowledges both the observable world of science and the more interior worlds of consciousness and spirit.

In the words of Fritjov Capra, author of *The Tao of Physics*, "...
we are in the midst of a paradigm shift; the old paradigm is the Cartesian, Newtonian world view, the mechanistic world view. The new paradigm is the wholistic, ecological world view. And we need this shift of
perception. Our society, our universities, our corporations, our econ-
omy, our technology, our politics are all structured according to the
old Cartesian paradigm. We need the shift."[10]

The shifting and revisioning of our attitudes, values and beliefs
into a new, holistic world-view involves movement along a number of
dimensions:

From		To
atomistic	>	holistic
dualistic	>	monistic
parochial	>	global
linear	>	mosaic
mechanistic forms	>	organic forms
independence	>	interdependence
competitive relations	>	collaborative relations
rationalization	>	responsibility
self-control	>	self-expression
separate objectives	>	linked objectives
masculine healing	>	androgenous healing
endurance of stress	>	capacity for joy
projection	>	introjection
attachment	>	attunement
ego-centered	>	life-centered
shizophysiology	>	synchrophysiology
achievement	>	self-actualization
having	>	being
self-image based on quantity of production	>	sense-of-self based on quality of experience

What a Body/Mind Psychology is telling us is that, given the degree of destruction, fragmentation, and confusion within our society,
this revolutionary shift toward a holistic, life-centered view of the entire body/mind/spirit complex may be a critical factor in undoing the
ever-tightening cocoon we've woven from our ancestral fears and fantasies.

Notes

1. Fox, Michael W. Body-Spirit-Being, In *Meditations With Animals*,
Gerald Hausman, 1986, Bear and Company, Santa Fe, New Mexico.

2. Sorokin, P. A. *The Crisis of Our Age*, 1941, Dutton, New York.

3. Vlahos, Olivia. *Body: The Ultimate Symbol*, 1979, J. B. Lippincott Co., New York.

4. Hausman, Gerald. *Meditations With Animals*, 1986, Bear and Company, Santa Fe, New Mexico.

5. Jaynes, Julian. *The Origins of Consciousness in the Breakdown of the Bi-Cameral Mind*, 1976, Houghton Mifflin, Boston.

6. Descartes, Rene. *Discourse on Methods and the Meditations* and *Rules for the Direction of Mind*, 1974, Penguin Classics, New York.

7. Lynch, James. *Utne Reader*, July, 1985.

8. Hebb, D. O. Drives and the Central Nervous System, *Psychological Review*, 1955, 62, 243.

9. Harman, Willis. *Global Mind Change: The Promise of the Last Years of the Twentieth Century*, 1988, Knowledge Systems, Inc., Indianapolis, Indiana.

10. Capra, Fritjov. The *Tao of Physics* Revisited, Renee Weber, In *The Holographic Paradigm and Other Paradoxes*, Ken Wilber, ed., 1982, New Science Library/Shambhala, Boston.

Suggested Readings

Capra, Fritjov. *The Tao of Physics*, 1975, Shambhala, Boston.

Capra, Fritjov. *The Turning Point*, 1982, Bantam, New York.

Graves, Florence. The New Age of Consciousness, 1989 Guide to New Age Living, *New Age Journal*. Boulder, Colorado.

Royce, Joseph. Metaphoric Knowledge and Humanistic Psychology, In *The Challenges of Humanistic Psychology*, James Bugental, ed., 1967, McGraw Hill, New York.

Royce, Joseph. *The Encapsulated Man*, 1965, Random House, New York.

Tart, Charles T. *PSI: Scientific Studies of the Psychic Realm*, 1977, E. P. Dutton, New York.

Wilber, Ken. *No Boundary*, 1981, New Science Library/Shambhala, Boston.

2

Talking Heads

ITEM: Melbourne, *Times of London*. A leading American surgeon claimed here today that human brain transplants are now medically feasible, but he said the whole head would probably have to be grafted at the same time. Professor David Hume, Chief of the Department of Surgery at the Medical College of Virginia and a pioneer of organ transplants, said ... that the donor of the brain in such an operation would, in fact, be the recipient, as the mind would take over the body to which it was grafted. The person whose brain was transplanted would retain his personality, as the brain is a memory bank, he said.[1]

Can there be any doubt that on a cultural level, as well as on an individual level, we occupy a world of extremely pronounced splits — between the flesh and blood biology of who we are, and the concepts and images of who we *think* we are.

Psychiatrist Alexander Lowen[2] believes that centuries of Cartesian dualism — of overvaluing the world of thoughts and concepts, while devaluing the body/mind experience — is producing a kind of schizoid, hyperconscious madness.

In the midst of this self-generated insanity, we each play the role of objective observer to all that our bodies perform — without *directly* experiencing our body's sensations, feelings and emotions. He states, "There is something crazy about a pattern of behavior that places achievement of success above the need to love and be loved. There is something crazy about a person who is out of touch with the reality of his or her being — the body and its feelings."

Psychiatrist Robert Hall believes that our attempt to avoid and deny the lived-body experience rests on our nightmarish fear of plunging into a painfully confused and blood curdling terror, where we are forced into awareness that our lives are temporary, and our existence is impermanent. "The contraction of fear," he states, "is turning to the safety of something as a safe place. We use a superstructure of images, beliefs and conditioned responses as a strategy. And our recoil from this knowledge of impermanence is felt *physically* — as a feeling of being clutched around the heart."[3]

Social psychologist Stanton Peele believes that our head-strong obsession with images and concepts, along with our compulsion to armor and defend against the lived-body, is a form of cultural addiction, comparable to an individual's addiction to alcohol, valium, or crack-cocaine.

Like the addict, we tend to view the lived-body as a source of pain, fear, and personal vulnerability and, likewise, we develop addictive cultural solutions for dealing with the potential panic.

Fear and feelings of inadequacy push the addicted to seek a constancy of stimulation and setting, rather than novel and spontaneous experiences. Similarly, we overvalue our language-games and ego-concepts, which appear to us as more predictable and controllable, while actively denying and repressing our body sensations, feelings and emotions. "If being detached from any kind of direct experience is harmful," Peele warns, "then detachment from the rhythms of our bodies is doubly so. Such an attitude influences everything we do."[4]

Hyper-Consciousness

The schism between body and mind, according to psychiatrist Ronald Laing,[5] produces a stressful state of *hyperconsciousness*, a state of *false-self*, in which we produce thoughts and images, and execute performance-strategies with increasing and unrelenting speed.

Cut off from its home, the disembodied false-self must root its very existence in the attitudes, opinions and beliefs that others hold of us at any particular time. As with the angels and demons of yesteryear, we helplessly depend on intermediaries to give a sense of meaning to our existence. After all is said and done, however, the false-self senses that this ground is made of sand, and the confusion and panic only mount as the grains of sand continue to weaken and fall away.

Faced with chronic anxiety and attacks of panic, we become *self-conscious* — increasingly obsessed with the experience of being policed by someone else, or by an illusory, split-off part of our selves which acts as monitor and judge of our performances: rational-irrational, acceptable-unacceptable, good-bad, sane-insane, and so on.

Immersed in a false-self system which changes as other's images of us shift and change, we become frantic and feel forced to turn others into "things." Disembodied ourself, we now rob others of their personhood—de-personalizing them into transparent stereotypes and objects of manipulation.

We are, of course, born into this world, and its body-of-knowledge becomes our own by the very fact of our participation in the world. And, yet, like the mythical Narcissus, we can become immersed in, and hypnotized by surface reflections when they have been cut off from their ground of meaning — the lived-body.

In its least distorted form, according to Lowen, disembodiment involves an inflation and obsession with our sexual image and prowess. We become self-absorbed, overly confident, arrogant, outwardly charming and, often, quite impressive to others.

At the other, more devastating, extreme, we lose all contact with the experience of lived-body, becoming increasingly anxious and paranoid — believing not only that people and/or demons are actually looking at us, or following behind, or talking about us — but are conspiring against us because we are very important, and, of course, very "special."[6]

In between these extremes, we find false-self engaged in various strategies, schemes, and manipulations, often caught in a knot of self-destructive behavior that eventually sabotages our lives. Struggling with feelings of inadequacy, devoid of a fully developed sense-of-self and meaningful relationships, we often compensate for these deficiencies by forming superficial friendships and focusing on empty lifestyles fueled by competition for success and status; or by resort to alcohol, drugs and impersonal sexual trysts. As the journey unfolds and the torment mounts, we become white-knuckled — confounding ourselves, as well as our friends, lovers and family.

Absorbed in false-self, we become, like the mythical Narcissus, prisoners in our own house of mirrors—acting out scenes in which the leading character is watching the leading character watching the leading character watching ... who?

> One is afraid of
> the self that is afraid of
> the self that is afraid of
> the self that is afraid
> One may perhaps speak of reflections
>
> R. D. Laing, *Knots*[7]

Samsara

To Eastern thinkers, to be immersed in the madness of hyper-consciousness is to suffer *samsara*.[8]

In samsara, we become increasingly obsessed with a kind of high-speed linear chain of thoughts and concepts fueled by an unremitting questioning process which, usually, begins with the question "WHY?", such as — why is this happening?

Each question leads to two or more answers, each of which leads to two or more questions — and so on, until we are swept into a conceptual vortex of photographic slide shows and holographic mind-movies. In terms of physical and psychological breakdown, this is the point where the snake bites its own tail, where the illusions takes their toll.[9]

From this Eastern perspective, samsara is experienced not so much as drowning, or falling, as a deadening claustrophobia caused by the lack of interior spaciousness. We feel shut off, blocked, armored and breathless. The proximity of events, the multiplicity of relationships, the intense pressure, the crammed packaging of our daily existence, continues to mount until we feel bloated, stressed—ready to explode or implode — into some slow-motion, self-immolating burn.

We seem to rub not only shoulders, but minds. No less important than our bodies, our minds feel trapped in containers with less and less space to move, to be alone, to rule over itself, to exist without constantly being affected, influenced, shoved around, persuaded, squeezed, propagandized, and trampled. The world appears increasingly heartless and cold, and we experience severe helplessness and dread at having to stomach the endless gulfs between ourself and others; ourself and nature; ourself and, truly, being-in-the-world.

This is the breaking point, the final stretch, where our disembodied fakeness is worn thin and made useless. This is the turning-point where the talking head, with its bit-by-bit storage system, and its overemphasis on past memories and future projections, must, either, break apart, or, actually, begin the search for embodied ways of being.

The ironical zen-twist, in all of this, is that the cataclysmic breakdown results, not so much from real, or even imagined attacks from out there, as from the devastation brought on by the defensive maneuvers of a mind in flight from its natural home — *the lived-body.*

You are in search of inner peace but you hate your body and senses. you long for inner joy but develop hostility towards the body which is a means to that joy, as though it were your most formidable enemy ...

Swami Muktananda, *Play of Consciousness*[10]

Embodied Being

Whether from the Eastern or Western perspective, many theorists agree that the experience of lived-body is of an entirely different order — and, yet, one which remains accessible to each of us in every moment.

Lived-body is experienced as *true self*, as being thoroughly and spaciously *aware* of one's embodiment from moment-to-moment — sensing precisely the body sensations, feelings, and thoughts which give form and meaning to each living moment. From the perspective of body/mind psychology, it is this experience of being grounded in the flesh and blood body which provides the precondition for an alternative set of possibilities as to how we live, love and heal ourselves.

As embodied beings, we are just as likely to experience the dangers that threaten the body; pain, decay and death, as we are to experience the pleasure, joy, and connectedness which grows from a clear sense of being embodied in-the-world. It by no means follows, however, that a person genuinely grounded in the lived-body is, automatically, an authentic and integrated person. After all, we still have to discover who we truly are. But participation in the lived-body, in returning us to the fundamentals of our body-of-knowledge, may provide us with a personal sense of wholeness and integrity in an increasingly heartless and disembodied world.

Notes

1. Roszak, Theodore. *Person/Planet*, 1978, Anchor Books, Garden City, New York.

2. Lowen, Alexander. *The Betrayal of the Body*, 1969, Collier-Macmillan, New York.

3. Hall, Robert. Fear, Violence, and the Body Experience (with Thomas Pope and Ron Boyer), *Lomi Papers*, Summer, 1980, Tomales, California.

4. Peele, Stanton. *Love and Addiction*, 1976, New American Library, New York.

5. Laing, Ronald D. *The Divided Self*, 1965, Pelican, New York.

6. Lowen, Alexander. *Nacissism: Denial of the True Self*, 1984, Macmillan, New York.

7. Laing, Ronald D. *Knots*, 1970, Pantheon Books, New York.

16   *Body of Knowledge*

8. Trungpa, Chogyam. *Cutting Through Spiritual Materialism*, 1973, Shambhala, Boston.

9. Tart, Charles T. Samsara: A Psychological View, In *Reflections of Mind: Western Psychology Meets Tibetan Buddhism*, Tarthang Tulku, ed., 1975, Dharma Publishing, Emeryville, California.

10. Muktananda, Swami. *Play of Consciousness*, 1978, Harper and Row, San Francisco.

Suggested Readings

Hanna, Thomas. *The Body of Life*, 1980, Knopf, New York.

Hanna, Thomas. *Bodies In Revolt: A Primer in Somatic Thinking*, 1972, Dell, New York.

Strozzi-Heckler, Richard. *The Anatomy of Change*, 1984, Shambhala, Boston.

Lowen, Alexander. *The Language of the Body*, 1971, Collier-Macmillan, New York.

Lowen, Alexander. *Bioenergetics*, 1975, Penquin, New York.

Mann, Richard D. *The Light of Consciousness*, 1984, SUNY Press, Albany, New York.

Trungpa, Chogyam. *The Myth of Freedom*, 1976, Shambhala, Boston.

Woodman, M. Psyche/Soma Awareness, *Quadrant*, 1984, 17, (2), 25–33.

3

Sigmund Freud and the Talking Cure

> There is nothing man fears more than the touch of the unknown. He
> wants to *see* what is reaching toward him, and to be able to recognize or
> at least to classify it. Man always tends to avoid physical contact with
> anything strange. In the dark, the fear of an unexpected touch can mount
> to panic. Even clothes give insufficient security: it is easy to tear them
> and pierce through to the naked, smooth, defenseless flesh of the victim.
> All the distances which men create around themselves are dictated by
> this fear.[1]
>
> —Elias Canetti, *Crowds and Power*

One of our most primitive fears is the fear of touch. Like our fears
of falling or suffocation, it probably evolved as a survival response
from our ancestral past. Touch from any unfamiliar source would
serve as our warning signal to either fight or flee—so as to avoid becoming injured or destroyed at the hands or claws of another.

According to Sigmund Freud, our earliest ancestors learned to
cope with these primal fears by projecting the internal psyche onto the
outer world. By way of this unconscious projection, which he termed
animism, our surrounding environment is experienced not only as
more familiar, but as an intimate part of our sense-of-self. The white
crane in the blue river — and all else that surrounds us, becomes one
and the same with who we are. Rather than struggling to dominate and
exert control over Nature, we embody the world, absorb it, as a seamless horizon. Lewis Mumford[2] describes this union of self and world in
this way: "Primitive man was sustained by a sense of union with his
world: stones, trees, animals, spirits, people, all spoke to him; and was
in them and of them."

This fundamental body/mind experience — this capacity to be at
one with the external world was, to Freud,[3] " ... the first conception of
the world which man succeeded in evolving which was therefore psychological." Ironically, by the time Freud stated his revolutionary
ideas, post-Victorian Europeans had become so alienated from the

lived-body and the natural world, that his ideas appeared radical to them — sometimes outrageously so.

The body, sexuality, and anything suggesting touch had, by then, become locked up tight as Queen Victoria's corset. And yet, for precisely the same reasons, it was a cultural climate ripe for Freud's seminal ideas. The dawn of the Machine Age, the collision between Science and Faith, spreading labor reform movements, European feminists demanding rights, and widespread intellectual unrest, all together, reflected a culture primed for fundamental change.

Today, however, Freud's formerly radical theories, about the structure and form of the human psyche, are very much a part of our Western body-of-knowledge. In fact, it would be difficult to reflect upon our contemporary culture without recognizing Freud's powerful contributions. Because of him, what were once considered to be maddened visitors from the realm of spirits and demons, the *maladies imaginaires*, are no longer considered to be imaginary. Instead, Freud's theory that our emotional pain and suffering spring from the deep unconscious; from emotional repression and denial; and from things sexual and taboo, is now taken for granted.

In the same way, Freud's concepts of "id," "ego," "superego," "libido," and a host of related notions are almost common knowledge today. In fact, it would be difficult to find in the history of ideas, including religious history, someone whose influence on the body-of-knowledge was so immediate, broad and deep as was the influence of Sigmund Freud. Yet, his contribution to Body/Mind Psychology remains both clouded and controversial. Much of Freud's basic *theory* rests on the assumption of body/mind unity. On the other hand, *psychoanalysis*, the practice of Freud's therapy, is built on a strict split between body and mind — and a taboo-like avoidance of touch.

Lived-Body in Freud's Theory

Fundamental to all of Freud's thinking is the assertion that the lived-body is the source of all experience. According to Freud, our basic drives and conflicts are played out through lived-body at each developmental stage: oral, anal, phallic, latent, and genital. Psychoanalyst Weston LeBarre[4] notes that, "Psychoanalysis is the first psychology to take seriously the whole human body as a place to live-in."

Freud's theory maintains that it is the body which is the source of our experience. In early life, for example, we react to pain and pleasure spontaneously. The firing of neurons instantly informs us that the stove is, indeed, very hot — and the cookie, very sweet, indeed! The object and its image are interembedded as our psyches absorb the surroundings and are at one with them.

In our increasing interplay with the world, however, we soon learn that real objects are much more rewarding than imagined objects: real cookies taste much better than holographic cookies. This shift to what Freud termed the *reality principle* involves our perceptions, learned behaviors and increasing bodily controls coming together to permit meetings with the real world, directly.

> What an interesting finger
>   let me suck it
> It's not an interesting finger
>   take it away

R. D. Laing, Knots[5]

We quickly learn that, in the real world, certain desires and actions are not permitted — and are routinely punished by others. Holding back, or *repressing* impulses and actions connected to pleasure gratification becomes necessary. We must now ask permission to receive a cookie, and raiding the cookie jar without permission results in humiliation and pain. The process of repression, thus, has expressed in it both the action potential to release the desired impulse, as well as the social injunction to hold it back.

Freud maintained that ongoing repression of opposing feelings and emotions creates an ever-intensifying pressure within the psyche which sometimes results in overflowing of this dammed energy into certain areas of the body. Unable to fully receive and contain the overabundance of energy, the body zone becomes numbed, pained or diseased. In this way, the original emotional conflict is converted into a physical disorder.

These *conversion reactions*, as Freud termed them, could be processed and cured through various emotional releases and verbal expressions of the nuclear conflict. This healing process, called *catharsis*, involved stirring buried memories of the conflict until they could be brought into conscious awareness, assimilated and accepted by the individual.

As development proceeds, according to Freud, our pain becomes increasingly emotional — and the mind must translate the pain in an effort to find some meaning in it. But, if the mind is incapable of sufficient objectivity, or knows too little about the translation of psychological pain, we turn to another person to guide us — better trained, perhaps, or at least more removed from the issues at hand. Thus,

Freud gave meaning to the practice of psychoanalysis and psychotherapy as an extension of this human striving to attach meaning to
painful experiences.

However, whether we attempt to glean meaning independently, or
with the guidance of a counselor or therapist, the pain and suffering
must be *translated* through the mind. Thus, to Freud, the mind's ex-
planations always remain one step removed from the primary experience itself. If, as the old Italian proverb maintains, *tradutori traditori*,
that is, that the translators are traitors, then the mind, too, may be a
traitor in the absence of the primary experience of lived-body.

The Talking Cure

While Freud's basic theory is founded on experiences of lived-
body and their repression, psychoanalysis, in contrast, relies almost
exclusively on the concept of mind and the analysis of language for its
working model.

Evolving as it did in post-Victorian Europe, psychoanalysis
strictly forbids touching the patient or any other form of physical intervention during the healing process — viewing such practices as im-
moral, unprofessional, and suspect given the risk of taking advantage
of the patient at a vulnerable point in the therapy.

Although this was the stated rationale Freud offered in defense
of the touch taboo, some contemporary Freudian scholars suggest
that it was Freud's desire to have his theories and practices accepted
by the European professional community which directed him to ex-
clude from psychoanalysis any therapeutic practice which might be
viewed as sexually-suggestive or controversial. In his early studies of
hysteria, Freud, himself, employed touch in his practices. Later, however, as when Sandor Ferenzi, one of Freud's closest psychoanalytic
friends and colleagues, began hugging his patients in reward for their
psychoanalytic breakthroughs, Freud loudly voiced disapproval of
this practice.

From the perspective of a Body/Mind Psychology, however, a profound question still remains unanswered, and it is this: if the body
does indeed originate and manifest disturbances of mind, as Freud
made so clear, then why have practices of counseling and psychotherapy continued to so conspicuously avoid anything having to do with
the body itself? Why, in our so-called liberated society is the practice
of physical touch so forbidden in virtually all forms of psychotherapeutic intervention?

The most obvious and straightforward answer to this question concerns *sex*. Touch, afterall, is generally assumed to be related to sex, if not synonymous with it, in our contemporary body-of-knowledge. And, yet, we know that sex is every bit as much a mental event as it is a physical activity. Sigmund Freud discovered this to be the case in the early days of his clinical practice when, to his utter astonishment, a woman patient threw her arms around him and tried to kiss him after a particularly moving psychoanalytic session. Other patients, too, had become filled with gratitude that didn't seem merited to Freud, while others had grown hostile or angry with him for no apparent reason.

In reflecting on these varied reactions by his patients, Freud reasoned that they were reexperiencing childhood situations and conflicts which involved projecting their love, anger, fear, or sexual longings onto him as a parental surrogate. To this phenomenon, he gave the name *transference*. And he was honest enough to acknowledge his reciprocal feelings and aroused desires in these situations—to which he gave the name *counter-transference*.

The important point, however, is that talk alone could arouse sexual longings and desires in both the client and the therapist. In fact, Freud allowed the patient's sexual longings and desires, along with a host of other issues, to exist and actually become an integral part of the psychoanalytic process. The *talking cure*, through free association and memory recall, sexually stimulates or angers the body of the patient and, through more talk, is manipulated and interpreted to the patient by the therapist in the healing process.

Having excluded the life of the body from its endeavor, however, it has been taken as an article of faith among contemporary psychoanalysts that insight alone is the crucial factor in therapeutic change — although embarrassing observations of people in treatment suggest that many who do achieve powerful insights into their dilemmas do not necessarily reveal a significant reduction in their miseries.[6]

To a Body/Mind Psychology, the capacity for the therapeutic process to emotionally arouse therapist and client is ever present — be it a purely "talking" therapy, or one of the many emerging therapies which involve bodily as well as mental change in the client. The real issue to be addressed, once we remove the smokescreen of the validity or invalidity of psychological healing practices, is our own attitudes toward the body and to touch; as well as our adherence to long-established professional principles and ethics.

From the point of view of an Embodied Psychology, body and mind exist on a continuum, just as do biology and psychology. As the findings of both empirical and clinical studies mount, it is clear that emotional pain and mental confusion stresses the body and plays an integral role in causing various disease states. In fact, experts in the field of psychosomatic medicine estimate that at least 50 percent of all physical diseases and ailments, from cancer to back pain, have a significant psychological basis. On the other hand, it is just as clear that physical deprivation, disease, physical abuse, sexual molestation, and chronic bodily pain play a central role in our mental and emotional lives.

From the viewpoint of a monistic, body/mind psychology, there exists both irony and paradox in any healing practice which focuses exclusively on one end of the body/mind continuum — at the expense of the other. This principle would apply to any medical intervention on the physical body which excludes concern for the psychological state of the patient and its role in the healing process; as well as to any psychological intervention into the emotional or cognitive state of the individual which excludes concern for the physical body and its role in the healing process.

We live in a society that has ripped human experience and behavior in two — thereby alienating many of us from the primary source of our own experience, from Nature and from each other. Is it any wonder that touch, too, has become such an alien activity?

Notes

1. Canetti, Elias. *Crowds and Power,* 1973, Continuum Publishing, New York.

2. Mumford, Lewis. *The Transformation of Man,* 1962, Collier Books, New York, p. 52.

3. Freud, Sigmund. *The Basic Writings of Sigmund Freud,* 1938, Random House, New York, p. 877.

4. Le Barre, Weston. Personality from a Psychoanalytic Viewpoint, *The Study of Personality: An Interdisciplinary Appraisal,* 1968, Holt, Rinehart and Winston, New York.

5. Laing, Ronald D. *Knots,* 1970, Pantheon Books, New York.

6. Rothstein, Arnold, ed. *How Does Treatment Help?: On the Modes of Therapeutic Action of Psychoanalytic Psychotherapy,* 1989, International Universities Press, New York.

Suggested Readings

Freud, Sigmund. *Collected Papers,* 1956, Basic Books, New York.

————. *New Introductory Lectures on Psychoanalysis,* 1949, Norton, New York.

————. *Civilization and Its Discontents,* 1962, Norton, New York.

Bettelheim, Bruno. *Freud and Man's Soul,* 1983, Alfred A. Knopf, New York.

Wollheim, Richard. *Sigmund Freud,* 1971, Viking Press, New York.

4

Wilhelm Reich and the Body Politic

He was a giant in our time, a man who went beyond the boundaries; a modern Dostoevsky, a Mesmer, a Blake — and in one sense, a Prometheus. Like those "madmen" he too stood between two worlds — between the world above, and the world below. He too had found that place within oneself where life comes and goes. That place where God and man could meet, but seldom do.

—James Wyckoff, *Wilhelm Reich*

Sigmund Freud's profound theories provide the skeleton for a Body/Mind Psychology: with a way of conceiving of how energy manifests in the person; how it becomes bound and repressed within; and how it might be released through the psychotherapeutic process. But, it was Freud's influence on his student, and then colleague, Wilhelm Reich, that shines as his most outstanding contribution to revisioning modern psychology.

Wilhelm Reich[1] was one of Freud's most promising and favored students. In 1922, Freud made him his first assistant. Later, Reich would be admitted to the prestigious Vienna Psychoanalytic Society under Freud's direction. And, yet, while a direct disciple of Freud, Reich would prove to be too much of an individualist to accept the complete dogma of Freudian psychology and play the role of unquestioning disciple which Freud so demanded of his followers.

By 1927, Reich had begun to question Freud's theory that neuroses originated in some sexual disturbance in childhood. Instead, he became increasingly convinced that neuroses were rooted in some form of disembodiment, and in a consequent lack of sexual satisfaction in life.

During this same period, Reich was becoming more deeply interested in the human body as a primary focus in psychotherapy and self-healing. Finally, the insight took form — that the body and mind are a single, functional unit. Rejecting the Cartesian split, he chose to view psychological, as well as physical disorders, as rooted in the intermix-

ture of body, mind, emotions, intellect, muscle, and bone — all belong-
ing to the disorder as a unified whole, just as they are all part of
healthy, vital human functioning.

Reich was well aware of how Freud's psychoanalysis, in order to
make itself an acceptable science, took great pains to avoid any practice that might create doubt and controversy. The "touch-sex" equation, so prevalent at the time, created just such a risk. Reich's clinical
experience, however, constantly brought the dilemma of the touch taboo to foreground — pointing to the futility, if not the hyprocrisy, of
such an injunction.

Reich's interest in the body as a part of the healing process deepened. Descriptions of muscular holding patterns and their relationship
to certain personality traits appeared repeatedly in his published
works. And he slowly came to believe that if, in some way, this muscular armoring of the body could be reduced or eliminated, neurotic
patterns could be more easily accessed and brought to completion.
But only slowly did Reich begin to break psychoanalytic taboos
against touch in therapy. Psychiatrist Myron Sharaf describes Reich's
first experiences in the use of bodywork:

> In the early years of his focus on the body, he limited himself
> largely to commenting on various spasms. Then gradually, in the
> late 1930s, he began more intensive use of touch to attack the
> body's armor directly and elicit emotions bound up in muscular
> spasms. He would press hard with his thumb or the palm of his
> hand on a particular segment of the body armor; the jaw, neck,
> chest, back, or thigh. Such pressure often stimulated an outburst
> of crying or rage.[2]

Reich reasoned that in health, energy flows through the body in a
smooth, four-beat pattern:

$$tension \rightarrow charge \rightarrow discharge \rightarrow relaxation$$

This pattern, according to Reich, was seen most clearly in health
and in the human orgasm response. In illness and sexual dysfunction,
however, the flow of energy is blocked in the body. The incomplete discharge, in turn, blocks and distorts natural feelings, emotions, sexual
fulfillment and, when chronic, provides the source of psychiatric disorder and psychosomatic disease.

Muscularly contracting the body in response to some stressful
event is a natural and temporary event.[3] As we step from a curb and

hear the screeching of car brakes, for instance, the four-beat pattern unfolds. We freeze on the spot; the pupils of our eyes grow extremely large; our shoulders rise to protect our head; the heart races and our breath is caught at the top of the chest. In that femtosecond, energy streams toward the brain and its perceptual/thought functions as we instantaneously evaluate and strategize ways to deal with this threat to our very existence. As the vehicle comes to a safe stop, however, the cascade of stress responses reverses its movement: we release a sigh of relief; the breath relaxes; the heart slows; and the fear subsides as our musculature softens and returns to normal.

When our lives become filled with stressful events, however, these same muscular contractions become chronic and permanent. At first, this armoring of the musculature allows us to repress our imme-diate feelings and emotions in service to our physical or psychological survival. When chronic and permanently armored, however, the blocked energy builds in intensity stressing the body/mind complex until it finally bursts through the weakest link—as psychosomatic dis-ease, chronic pain and emotional dysfunction.

Reich[4] noted that muscles are arranged in segments across the longitudinal axis of the body and correspond to certain forms of emo-tional expression. The human body, of course, naturally functions as a single unit in expressing emotion. But when one muscle segment be-comes chronically armored, it blocks impulses to both itself and other segments — and since most emotional expression involves more than one segment of muscle, the impairment of one necessitates impair-ment in others. These six muscles segments included:

1. *Ocular Segment:* involves the eyes, forehead, and nose, and functions in the expression of anxious anticipation, fright, ag-gressiveness, suspiciousness, and crying.
2. *Oral Segment:* involves mouth, jaw, and lips, and functions in the emotional expression of crying, biting, sucking, and gri-macing.
3. *Throat Segment:* involves throat, neck, and Adam's apple, and functions in expression of deep sobbing, shouting, screaming, and spite.
4. *Chest Segment:* involves upper and middle chest, shoulders and arms, and functions in the expression of anger, longing, restraint, fear, rage, and frustrations in love relationships.
5. *Diaphragmatic Segment:* involves the entire breathing mech-anism, especially the diaphragm, and functions to control the intensity of all emotions — including extreme fear and plea-sure.

6. *Pelvic Segment:* involves the pelvis, genitals, buttocks, and legs, and functions especially in expressing sexuality, including sexual disturbances, such as lack of sensitivity, sexual rage, or anxious sexuality.

In his book, *Character Analysis,*[5] Reich concluded that the physical armoring of the body is functionally identical with certain defensive traits in the personality make-up of the individual. This parallel armoring of the personality, according to Reich, " ... served to protect the individual against pain, but also served to restrict severely the capacity for pleasure."

After decades of clinical research on the association of body structure and tension patterns with mental attitudes and beliefs, Reich concluded that the personality is composed of our habitual patterns of response to various situations; including conscious attitudes and values, styles of behaving (aggressiveness, shyness, etc.), posture, and physical habits of holding and moving the body.

In later years, Reich developed many bodywork techniques aimed at loosening the muscles of the chest and, thereby, enhancing the breathing process. One technique involves breathing fully and deeply, completely filling the lungs and then completely releasing the breath as the muscles of the chest and diaphragm are softened and loosened through deep pressure applied by the therapist. Breathwork, Reich noted, not only stimulates the release of repressed emotions, but often retrieves the originating memory: the traumatic and, often, infantile event associated with initiating the repression process in the first place. He states, " ... every muscular rigidity contains the history and meaning of its origin ... the armor itself is the form in which the infantile experience continues to exist as a harmful agent."

Reich viewed the body's natural, rhythmic flow of energy as the basis for health and happiness. The free movement of our breath and the undulations of our sexual feelings — without guilt, without compulsion, without tension, and without imposed morality were, to Reich, pathways to personal health, joy, and loving contact with one another.

His public pronouncements on the need for a free and loving approach to sexuality, along with his political leanings toward socialism eventually led to his imprisonment and death in the Federal Penitentiary at Lewisberg, Pennsylvania on November 3, 1957.

Body Politic

Throughout the remainder of his life, Wilhelm Reich struggled for the freedom of sexual expression — long before it became popular to do so. Decades before the Kinsey Report and Master's and Johnson's famous sexual studies, Reich noted our tendency to split love from sexuality; to separate the experience of lived-body from the world of thoughts, images and concepts of self and other. Reich viewed commercialized pornography and repressive religious moralism as two sides of the same coin and he wanted no part of either.

He was one of the few who envisioned the interconnectedness of things. He saw that there were no real boundaries — only arbitrary labels separating science from art, body from mind, and each individual from loving contact with self and others. He believed that the human body was inherently bound up with the meaningful, in the same way that God could be a function of natural laws and processes. And, he understood, that as dissolution or breakdown occurs, freedom for growth is also born.

Commenting on Reich's lifework, Psychiatrist David Boadella writes, "His entire work-effort was dedicated to exploring ways, whether therapeutic, educational, or social, of overcoming this basic split, and to helping people to lead more integrated lives in which the head and body spoke the same language as the heart."[6]

Reich's theory and approach to psychotherapy was a radical departure from Freud's psychoanalysis. He was, in fact, a leading pioneer in the field of psychosomatic medicine and body-oriented psychotherapy. And yet, much of his work was not taken seriously at first. Part of the reason may be attributed to the unsoundness of some of his riskier experiments; part to the somewhat romantic and sexually suggestive terms he coined to describe his psychology, such as orgonomy and orgiastic potency; and part to Reich himself, and his revolutionary belief that society itself is partially responsible for disembodying its own children and, thereby, contributing to their pain and suffering.

In his final years, Reich had increasing difficulties with authority, culminating in one of the strangest, most bizarre episodes of authoritarian reaction against one lone individual.

One of Reich's riskier experiments involved tests of an "orgone accumulator" — a small room constructed of layers of organic materials separated by sheet metal which was thought to trap high levels of "orgone energy." The question of whether this dense energy might play a role in the treatment of psychosomatic diseases, such as cancer, intrigued Reich and his students. It also intrigued Federal investigators who made use of the accumulator as the centerpiece of their case against Reich and his associates.

On February 10, 1954, the United States Food and Drug Administration delivered a twenty-seven page complaint against the Wilhelm Reich Foundation to stop all research studies and to cease and desist from all publications of Reich's writings. Reich refuted the jurisdiction of the court and was found guilty, not of the charges pending, but of "contempt of court." He was sentenced to two years in a federal penitentiary and a $10,000 fine. He died there, discredited, his materials burned or confiscated, his foundation a financial shambles—one more victim of the right-wing witch hunts of the McCarthy era.

There are those who believe that Reich went mad at the end. Others view him as a tormented visionary. In either case, it makes little difference. Nietzsche went "mad," Jonathon Swift went mad, and Oscar Wilde was declared mad. But in the long-run, the act of labeling them mad in no way weakened their impact on our ever-changing body-of-knowledge. So, too, in the case of Wilhelm Reich. Today, more than three decades after his death, his humanistic views of the whole person are taken seriously throughout the Western world, while his theories and therapeutic techniques supply the very tissue to a body/mind psychology.

Notes

1. Boadella, David, ed. *In the Wake of Reich*, 1977, Ashley Books, New York.

2. Sharaf, Myron. *Fury on Earth*, 1983, St. Martins Press, New York.

3. Reich, Wilhelm. *Selected Writings*, 1960, Farrar Strauss Cudahy, New York.

4. ———. *The Function of the Orgasm*, 1961, Noonday Press, New York.

5. ———. *Character Analysis*, 1933, Orgone Institute Press, Ansonia Station, New York.

6. Boadella, David. *Wilhelm Reich: The Evolution of His Work*, 1973, Henry Regnery Co., Chicago.

Suggested Readings

Baker, Elsworth. *Man in the Trap*, 1967, Macmillan, New York.

Mann, W. Edward and Edward Hoffman. *The Man Who Dreamed of Tomorrow: A Conceptual Biography of Wilhelm Reich*, 1974, Farrar, Straus & Giroux, New York.

5

The Neo-Reichians

> The principle of therapy is quite simple: merely to remove the chronic contraction which interferes with the free flow of energy throughout the organism and thus restore natural functioning. In practice, it may be extremely difficult.[1]
> — Elsworth Baker, *Man In the Trap*

The direct descendent of Wilhelm Reich is Elsworth Baker. Trained as a psychiatrist, his close association with Reich began in 1946, as an assistant in Reich's laboratory, and ended at his deathbed in Lewisberg Federal Penitentiary in 1957. Given the situation of his imprisonment, according to Psychiatrist Myron Sharaf,[2] "Reich conveyed a sense of 'the end' to Baker in their last meeting ... and asked him at that meeting if Baker would assume responsibility 'for the future of orgonomy'."

Elsworth Baker

For an entire decade following the death of their mentor, Elsworth Baker and colleagues practiced and taught a pure form of Reichian therapy, often against hostile or unsympathetic attitudes from the orthodox medical community. The decade culminated in the publication of Baker's theoretical guidebook to Reichian theories and practices, entitled, *Man In the Trap*.[3] One year later, in 1968, Baker founded the semiannual *Journal of Orgonomy*[4] and, later, the College of Orgonomy in Princeton, New Jersey. Through his efforts, the body of Reich's work was raised from the ashes.

Could Elsworth Baker have guessed that in the span of his own lifetime, his act would be viewed as a sort of "heart transplant"—from the dying body of Reich's work to a newer, expanding body-of-knowledge. It is safe to say that today, little more than thirty years following his death, Reich's work has been fully resuscitated.

Similarly, in the literary world, the benefits of Reich's ideas have been reaped. Nobel Prize winner Saul Bellow, who underwent Reichian therapy in the 1940s, was so enthusiastic about it that at least two of his works reveal a heavy influence of Reich's ideas. These are *The Adventures of Augie March* and *Henderson the Rain King*. Norman Mailer was also influenced by Reich's concepts and made use of them in *Advertisements for Myself*, in 1976.

Baker and colleagues, though dedicated to maintaining the purity of Reich's original theory and therapy, also extended and expanded his work. Baker, for one, although agreeing with the basic psychoanalytic framework of Reich's theories, nevertheless, differs with Reich on a number of interesting points. For example, Baker agrees that when armored muscles are freed, emotions connected to the original conflict are often elicited. However, Baker notes that when muscular armoring is the result of long-term authoritarian attitudes and actions which were pervasive events in our life, freeing the musculature may not release a particular memory of the event. He states that, " ... the lack of memories is connected to the fact that the adopted attitudes are implied, unspoken prohibitions imposed, gradually, at each stage of development."[5]

Based on his clinical observations of people's responses to touch, Baker also expanded the definition of *armoring*, itself, the term used by Reich to refer to chronically contracted muscles. Pleasant skin sensations, Baker notes, are not felt in heavily armored muscles — only deep pressure is registered by these muscle fibers. Newer and lighter armoring of the muscle, on the other hand, is experienced as unpleasantly ticklish to the touch.

Baker also gives great emphasis to the effects of armoring in the small muscles of the eyes. The eyes, according to Baker, are concerned with all distant contacts we make with the outer world and are most often the first to be traumatized and armored in response to some childhood terror or abuse.

Once armored, "hardened eyes" create increasingly distorted perceptions until, in the extreme, we may lose all depth perception, as well as the capacity for accurate reality testing. Lacking a depth of context for our perceptions, we become fueled by fear of our own cyclonic thoughts and emotions. In time, we begin to see only hate, anger, fear, and confusion in the eyes of others — and the hallucinations and delusions associated with the partial or total loss of contact with the body/mind experience take over our conscious world.

Although Baker agrees with Reich that a healthy and satisfying sexual life is an important means of releasing energy bound in the body/mind complex, he maintains that other physical activities, such as work and physical exercise, can also release bound-up energy. In fact, Baker views the developmental process itself, from conception to adolescence, as a process involving the release of bound energy. Baker's insight that release of bound energy is not exclusively a sexual matter provided the groundwork for a synthesis of ideas from various areas, including Gestalt Psychology, physical therapies, psychosomatic medicine, phenomenology, states of consciousness research, and Eastern disciplines.

Alexander Lowen

Unlike Elsworth Baker, who remained a dedicated "Reichian" in the fullest sense, another of Reich's prized students would come to play out the rejection of Reich — just as Reich had played out the rejection of his mentor, Sigmund Freud.

Alexander Lowen began his break from Reich when Reich began to concentrate, almost exclusively, on bodywork — at the expense of other equally important facets of the client's life. Retaining the basics of the psychoanalytic framework, Lowen's quest was for a more balanced approach to a Body/Mind Psychology — one which placed equal emphasis on psychological, social, *and* bodily processes.

Lowen's[6] approach, termed Bioenergetic Analysis, begins with the basic Reichian principle that all organisms are energetic processes which take in and release energy. He then proceeds to weave elaborations and extensions of this principle to the many aspects of our lives.

The taking in of energy, according to Lowen, builds up tension within us which, in its most extreme form, is experienced as deep pain. When this heightened tension is released, however, it is experienced as pleasure — and in the extreme, as pure ecstasy.

The charging up with energy takes place primarily in the upper body — the chest, the arms, and the head as breathing, eating, sensing, and thinking. The discharge of energy primarily involves the lower half of the body — the abdomen, pelvis, and legs as digestion, sexual release, physical movement, and a sense of groundedness to the earth.

The upward charge of energy, according to Bioenergetic theory, is toward the power-strivings of ego — prediction, power, and control. To be "hung up" or "up-tight" is to be immersed in narcissism and *samsara* — lacking contact with the body/mind experience, the *ground*. This results from muscularly blocking the flow of energy in the upper half of the body by overvaluing head-eye knowledge, at the expense of the heart. As did his teacher before him, Lowen asserts that

our society bears significant responsibility for creating disembodiment and neurotic conditions by training its children to gather and
overvalue the images, things and symbols won by way of a power striving ego.

Bioenergetic therapists use many of Reich's catharsis techniques, especially those involving enhancement of the flow of breath in
the body. Other exercises and stress-postures are directed toward tap-
ping the body's natural tendency to vibrate, especially in the process
of mobilizing formerly blocked energy.

Stanley Keleman,[7] a neo-Reichian who founded the Center for Energetic Studies, in Berkeley, California, has extended and advanced the
use of Bioenergetic exercises and stress-postures in his many books
and monographs. He demonstrates the use of a kicking exercise, in this
way:[8]

> Lie down on your back with your shoes off. Now begin to kick the
> bed. Start with raising your legs to right angles to your body so
> that they go straight up in the air toward the ceiling. Then bring
> them straight down, hitting the bed with your heels. Keep kick-
> ing, always lifting your legs at right angles to your body. Begin to
> feel what the emotional experience is as well as the action.
>
> What is the image that you have as the readiness to kick?
> What is the way that you kick? Is your kicking heavy? Is it
> light ... ? ... as you begin to kick, you will discover that internal
> events—memory, excitement—begin to form the kicking into an-
> other experience, into angry kicking or despairing kicking or
> gleeful kicking. We have entered into that place where we kick in
> response to our internal environment. Here is the challenge of
> forming ourselves in relationship to new messages, to a new state
> or attitude toward the world.

Grounding, a series of unique exercises developed by Lowen and
colleagues, involves contacting the opposite of being "up-tight"—that
is, the experience of being *in* the lived-body, aware of the ground, in
contact with and "under-standing" the here and now. In so doing, according to Lowen, we reestablish a personal ground-of-meaning to our
psychological life; and the experience of pleasure, relaxation, and psychological security to our social life. This downward discharge of energy, according to Lowen, is directed toward the biological strivings of
embodiment, belongingness, love, and the experience of stillness in
our lives.

Fritz Perls

Fritz Perls is honored as the founder of Gestalt psychotherapy and as a powerful contributor to both the theory and practice of body/ mind psychotherapy. His unique view of unconscious processes, and use of his quick and powerful therapeutic techniques are essential ingredients in the emerging paradigm.

The principles of Gestalt psychology had their beginnings, in the early 1900s, in the perceptual experiments conducted by Kohler and Wertheimer in Germany. These studies revealed that the human perceptual system has a propensity to form patterns or meaningful configurations called *gestalts* — even when the sources of stimulation were, themselves, incomplete. A partial circle, for instance, is still perceived as a circle.

Years of subsequent research in human learning, motivation and social psychology revealed the same phenomenon in these areas. Navy men stationed in the Arctic, for example, who had not eaten meat or socialized with women for many months, would not, when allowed to view photographs for only milliseconds, perceive a chair or a window, but *would* perceive a photograph of a steak or a nude woman. Or in other studies, when a class of students was split into two groups and tested, the group that had *not* completed the test could remember the test, the testers, and the circumstances over time, while those who had completed the test had greater difficulty remembering this information. The results made clear that we are driven to complete incomplete experiences. And that, until completed, unfinished experiences cause us to seek completion perceptually, emotionally, and cognitively.

Gestalt Psychology developed into an empirically-validated protest against the attempt to study and understand human nature by exclusively analytic means. The Gestalt research established that our experiences, even when atomized and fragmented, always attempt to pattern themselves in some meaningful way. Our experiences are more than the sum of their parts — and the "more" is the pattern or configuration which strives for completion and meaning.

Fritz Perls was greatly influenced by Gestalt Psychology and Freud's psychoanalytic theory early in his career. In the 1940s, Perls entered into psychoanalysis with Wilhelm Reich in Germany. Later in life, Reich's theories of armoring and the functional identity of body/ mind played major roles in his thinking. In fact, after Freud, Reich is the most frequently referenced author in Perls'[9] classic work, *Ego, Hunger and Aggression*.

Perls' major contributions to a body/mind psychology were to extend Gestalt principles to psychotherapy and to the study of psychological process; and to demystify psychotherapy by insisting that the experiential world of the individual could be best understood through the individual's own unique description of that world.

In his basic theory of the human psyche, Perls replaced the Freudian psychoanalytic model, with its emphasis on the unconscious as a dark and tangled ocean of sexual impulses and aggressive instincts, with a theory which maintains that the source of our conflicts and frustrations is not so much the "ocean" of the unconscious, as the "bubbles" of *unfinished business* which push to the surface of our consciousness and effect every thing we do.

Simply put, situations (potential gestalts) in our lives, which are in some way unfinished or incomplete, create tension in our memory which then rises to the center of our perceptual/emotional/conceptual modes of experience where they exert an ongoing stressful influence— until completed. Perls' Gestalt Psychotherapy involves numerous techniques directed toward facilitating the individual to finish unfinished business: the anger never fully expressed to the scolding parent; the grief never completely expressed at the death of a loved one; the screams of terror never fully convulsed in the dark nightmare, and so on.

Psychologist James Kepner,[10] in his book *Body Process*, notes that although Perls accepted Reich's formulation of the "functional identity" of body and mind, his concern was more with the individual's experience of the body and its role in forming the sense-of-self. He states that, "For Perls the first step was concentration on body sensation to restore the body sense of the client, and *then* to undo muscular repression." Unlike Reich who viewed muscular armoring as a defense that impeded therapy, Perls viewed muscle tension as a part of the sense-of-self, albeit, one that is disowned and unaware.

In addition to working with lived-body experiences through body awareness and concentration, Perls' methodology, like Reich's, places great emphasis on breathing, posture, stance, and nonverbal expression of repressed feelings and emotions.

Robert Hall

Robert Hall,[11] a student and, then, colleague of Perls; and a psychiatrist also trained in Eastern psychology, as well as the Rolfing bodywork technique, extended Perls' powerful insights into new realms. Hall reasoned that, given that the body and mind are functionally identical, then the "unfinished business" of which Perls spoke, must also extend into particular muscles of the body, itself, where it exerts an ongoing influence. For the business to be truly finished, blocked energy must be released from these muscles of the body and be permitted to express itself as various forms of movement.

In concert with colleagues, Alyssa Hall, Richard Strozzi-Heckler, and Katherine Flaxman, Hall founded the Lomi School. Named for the ancient Hawaiian method of deep muscle massage, Lomi Work brought to the Gestalt framework various forms of bodywork; Reichian breathwork; body education techniques; Eastern spiritual practices, including Vipassana meditation and hatha yoga; and, the ancient martial arts of Aikido and Tai Chi Chu'an. (See chapter 6.)

The work of Robert Hall et al, opened the way to a new synthesis which challenges not only the old duality of body-mind, but all the old dualities of East-West, masculine-feminine, and Science-Art. The work of the Lomi School, originating in California, gradually spread to Western Europe during the 1970s and 1980s, where it continues to thrive.

> The body is the tapestry woven from the commerce between experience, mind, and connective tissue. When these parts are not in conscious, harmonious interplay, there is a residue of unprocessed information. Perls called this 'unfinished business.' This unprocessed information is dispatched to various parts of the body where it eventually begins to mark the structure of the organism, which in turn affects its function. This promotes a closed system that prohibits the individual from experiencing the action of the present moment.
>
> (Richard Strozzi-Heckler *The Anatomy of Change*)[12]

Notes

1. Baker, Elsworth. *Man In the Trap*, 1967, Macmillan, New York.

2. Sharaf, Myron. *Fury On Earth*, 1983, St. Martins Press, New York.

3. See n. 1 above.

4. *Journal of Orgonomy*, Orgonomic Publications, Inc., New York.

5. See n. 1 above.

6. Lowen, Alexander, *Bioenergetics*, 1975, Penquin Books, New York.

7. Keleman, Stanley, *Your Body Speaks Its Mind*, 1976, Pocket Books, New York.

8. ———. *Somatic Reality*, 1979, Center Press, Berkeley.

9. Perls, Frederick S. *Ego, Hunger and Aggression*, 1969, Vintage Books, New York.

10. Kepner, James. *Body Process*, 1987, Gestalt Institute of Cleveland Press, Cleveland (p. 214).

11. Hall, Robert. *The Lomi Papers*, 1979, Tomales, California.

12. Strozzi-Heckler, Richard. *The Anatomy of Change*, 1984, Shambhala, Boston.

Suggested Readings

Hatcher, Chris and Philip Himelstein, eds. *The Handbook of Gestalt Therapy*, 1983, Jason Aronson, New York.

Royak-Shaler, Renee, and Jeffrey A. Schaler. Lomi Body Work as Gestalt Therapy, *Journal of Holistic Medicine*, 1980, 2 (2), 127–36.

6

Screamers, Beamers, and Assorted Dreamers

... we have ... the psychoanalytic, the transactional ... There are the Rei-
chians, the neo-Reichians, the Rolfers, the Alexander and Feldenkrais
people, and the hypnotists. There are the existentialists, Rogerians,
transactional analysts, behaviorists and the laser beamers who offer
change for the price of a short trip through one's neurolinguistic soft-
ware. ... They are all here ... [1]

—Joseph C. Zinker, *Body Process*

From the perspective of Body/Mind Psychotherapy, the theoretical position to which one adheres, and the methodology one employs
matters only in that they are effective in healing; in removing energetic
blocks to creativity and growth; and, in relieving the sense of personal
claustrophobia. As the old body-mind duality continues to collapse,
various attempts are being made to create blends of what were formerly purely physical or purely mental methods of healing. In this
sense, be they blends of Freudian, Reichian, neo-Reichian, Gestalt,
Bioenergetic, Lomi, meditation, autogenic training or behavioral anesthesiology, what *works* is what matters.

There are many healing practices which emphasize body/mind
integration as their core goal. In surveying some of these practices, it
is clear that some place greater emphasis on either the body *or* the
mind and are sometimes lacking a strong basis in theory and empirical
research. Many rest on some Eastern philosophical system, or at least
recognize the need for some philosophical middle ground, such as
Taoism, to facilitate the blending of diverse perspectives into a holistic
paradigm.

What follows is a sampling of some additional methods and approaches participating in creating a new body/mind psychotherapy.

Acupuncture, Acupressure, and Shiatsu

These, and similar methods, based on ancient Chinese theories
and body maps, employ needle or finger stimulation of pressure points

on the body. They have traditionally been used to facilitate physical healing of various disorders, control of physical pain, and, most recently, in control of addictive urges in substance abusers.[2]

According to the Peking Acupuncture Anesthesia Coordinating Group,[3] newer research suggests that acupuncture and acupressure techniques act to enhance the responsiveness of the immunological system as seen in the number of white blood corpuscles and the intensity of phagocytosis following treatment.

In research on the role of these techniques in controlling bodily pain, it is interesting to note that stimulation of a body point has bilateral analgesic effects. Thus, in knee surgery, for instance, it was shown that stimulation of points on the healthy leg produced anesthesia in the opposite leg. Such research lends support to Reich's assertions regarding the segmental structure of the body. In addition, published reports by the Shanghai Acupuncture Anesthesia Coordinating Group show that the impulses for anesthesia are transmitted mainly through deep muscles of the body.

In comparing acupuncture and acupressure, a series of animal experiments conducted at Peking Medical College found that needle stimulation of specific points produced a rise of 128 percent in the pain threshold while finger pressure stimulation produced a rise of 133 percent, suggesting that they are equally effective in certain applications.

Massage

There are many massage methods with great variation in emphasis: from stimulation of the circulatory and immunological systems (Petrissage, Bindegewebmassage);[4] to release of blocked energy in the musculature (Japanese, Chinese); to relaxation and sensual stimulation (Esalen, Swedish, British).

Records reveal that massage was practiced as early as 3000 B.C. by the Chinese. *The Cong Fau of Tao-Tse*, an ancient Chinese text, contains lists of massage techniques and exercises used to promote healing. One such technique, called *amma*, involves rubbing and pressing specific points on the body. The amma method entered Japan around the sixth century A.D. as *shiatsu* and involves pressing points on the body called *tsubo* to release bound energy and improve circulation.

Artifacts reveal that virtually every culture studied, including Persian, Greek, and Roman, as well as modern cultures, employ some form of massage. Beginning with Hippocrates, the father of Western medicine, and extending to contemporary nursing practices, massage is an integral part of medical healing practices undergoing a Renaissance. This renewal of interest in massage extends to *sports massage*, a method of massage especially developed to prepare athletes for upcoming events and to aid in the body's regenerative and restorative capacities following rigorous competition or actual injuries.

The *Trager Method*, developed by Milton Trager, uses movements called *mentastics*, gentle shaking movements of different parts of the body which releases pent-up tensions. Particularly gentle in its approach, the Trager Method is especially useful in stress-reduction and immunoenhancement programs involving the elderly.

Other methods of massage include *reflexology*, which focuses particular attention on the hands and feet, and *touch for health*, a simplified method of applied kinesiology which focuses on principles of movement as applied to the human anatomy.[5]

Massage has become an integral part of multimodal healing programs, not only because of its many benefits in stress reduction, pain abatement, and circulation enhancement, but also because of its role in treating acute touch starvation. Gay Luce,[6] Director of SAGE (Senior Actualization and Growth Exploration) describes some of the techniques used in work with the elderly:

> We did a number of exercises and used a very eclectic approach. We used Alexander-method techniques for mindfulness of the spinal column. We did body sensing, listening to sounds through the body, getting used to physical contact. We started doing a lot of massage. This is very important, because touch is an essential source of emotional nourishment ... if you live in isolation and nobody touches you anymore, there is a message that is lacking in your life ...

Polarity Therapy

Based on the theories of Randolph Stone,[7] this approach emphasizes a particular view of the flow of energy in the body based on the Eastern theory of *chakras*. The method attempts to balance the flow of energies through diet, stress exercises, and the balancing of somatic pressure points through therapeutic touch.

Stone's concept of "polarity" is similar to the two poles of yin and yang in Taoism and the balance of these energies is sought in each chakra: *head chakra* in psychic awareness and spirituality; *throat chakra* in communication; *heart chakra* in compassion and caring;

naval chakra in the use of power and will by the individual; *genital chakra* in emotional drive and sexual expression; and *root chakra*, in physical survival patterns. In the healthy person, according to Stone, energy is in balance in all aspects of the person's life—physical, emotional, mental and spiritual.

Rolfing

Founded by Ida Rolf,[8] this approach has, for many years, been viewed as a quick and effective technique of postural realignment involving deep stretching and restructuring of the fascial tissue surrounding the muscles of the body. In her later writings, Rolf paid increasing attention to psychological processes and emotional release and, consequently, Rolfers are becoming increasingly attuned to these more subtle realignments. Generally speaking, however, psychological processing remains peripheral to basic Rolfing theory and training.

Meditation

In its many and diverse forms, including zen, Morita and transcendental,[9] meditation reduces the activity of the sympathetic nervous system — this is the part of the nervous system which prepares the body for stressful emergencies. Meditation produces a lower rate of metabolism, a reduction in heart and respiratory rates, and also decreases blood lactate levels, a chemical linked to stress. Meditation has also been shown to increase alpha brain wave activity and reports of relaxed wakefulness.[10]

A number of studies have found that a high percentage of meditators who used drugs stopped or decreased their use through meditation. Wallace and Benson,[11] for example, found that among people who meditated using transcendental meditation (TM), drug use fell from 78 percent to 22 percent. Other effects of meditation include increased body and sensory awareness, strong emotions, and a sense of timelessness.

Vipassana Meditation

Vipassana or *insight* meditation has been an integral part of Tibetan Buddhist practices for nearly three millennia. Unlike most meditation practices, whose goal is the achievement of a state of relaxation, this approach to meditation emphasizes body awareness and detachment from our neurotic, ego-based connections to sensations, feelings, thoughts and, concepts.[12]

One variation of Vipassana meditation, called Maitri, combines meditation with particular body postures assumed in five rooms varying in color and shape. Based on the Tibetan theory of personality, each room and posture is meant to intensify a particular neurotic tendency so it might be more easily processed in meditation. Interestingly, Tibetan Buddhist principles and practices, born in near-total isolation, appear to play an increasingly important role in the emerging body/mind paradigm.

Yoga

This ancient Hindu practice may be the earliest and most complete system of body/mind integration. The elements of yoga were already published in the *Vedas*, circa 3,000 – 2,000 B.C.

As usually practiced, yoga involves the assumption of various postures, called *asanas*, and awareness of the body sensations created as various muscles are stretched and extended. All yoga exercises comprise a unique, eight-stage method. The first five form stages of *purification;* the following two involve spiritual enlightenment and achievement of the ecstatic state of *samadhi;* and the last one is a stage of *aloneness* in which the mind is absorbed in consciousness. Often, directed self-suggestion is practiced by means of verbal *mantras* which are repeated during asanas. This is similar to methods used by certain Christian adepts involving concentrated awareness on the region of the heart while certain prayers are repeated in tune with the heartbeat while breathing rhythmically.

Yoga, like other movement arts (e.g., Aikido, Tai Chi Chu'an) is traditionally practiced as a means of promoting a *state* of consciousness akin to enlightenment. Unlike Vipassana meditation which seeks to facilitate psychological processes, most forms of yoga view the body as a vehicle to induce states of spiritual rapture and serenity. The yogis capacity to control breathing rate, heart rate, pain and other autonomic processes has often been described as "miraculous" by the uninformed.[13]

Biofeedback

Considered by many to be the "yoga of the West," biofeedback involves electronic amplification of various physiological processes, such as heart rate, pulse rate, and muscular tension signals which are fed back to the individual who learns to bring them under voluntary control by way of a self-induced state often described as *relaxed awareness*. This state manifests as slow, synchronous, evenly modulated electrical activity in the brain called *alpha activity*.

Numerous research studies make clear that what appear to be other-than-worldly feats of Eastern yogis and fakirs, such as lying on a bed of nails or firewalking, consistently involve self-induction of the alpha state of brain activity. Like yoga, biofeedback induces a state of consciousness rather than psychological processing. Biofeedback is especially effective in the treatment of stress-related disorders, such as migraine headache, and in the control of chronic pain.[14]

Feldenkrais Method

Developed by Israeli philosopher Moshe Feldenkrais,[15] this theory, both simple and profound, holds that each individual's sense of self is composed of a constellation of physical, emotional and intellectual habit patterns which can become limiting and restrictive. The Feldenkrais Method involves the use of various physical exercises meant to extend and expand the restrictive boundaries of self.

Behavioral Anesthesiology

This very recent development extends traditional forms of chemical anesthesia to include music, visualization, touching, relaxation training and verbal and nonverbal communication signals presented to the patient preoperatively, during surgery and during postoperative recovery. With careful titration of drugs, emotional support and psychological care, these techniques allow the patient to participate more fully in the surgical procedure and increase the chances of a successful recovery.[16]

Autogenic Training

This comprehensive relaxation technique was developed in Europe by Schultz and Luthe and includes six basic inducement exercises: heaviness, warmth, cardiac regulation, respiration, abdominal warmth, and cooling of the forehead. It also includes seven meditation experiences: spontaneous experience of colors, experience of selected colors, visualization of concrete objects, visualization of abstract objects, experience of selected states of feeling, visualization of other persons, and answers from the unconscious. Although it requires considerable time to master completely, autogenic training is proving to be a powerful regimen in stress-reduction and immunoenhancement programs.[17]

Numerous methods have been developed using combinations of relaxation training, imagery, visualization, meditation, self-hypnosis, and sensory awareness. Many methods, such as those developed by Simonton, Clynes, Schacter and Selver, are playing an ever-increasing role in behavioral medicine and psychosomatic treatment programs.[18]

The Alexander Technique

This movement reeducation technique was developed by the Austrian therapist, F. Matthias Alexander. Similar to Reich's basic theory, Alexander maintained that muscular tensions and blocks in the body are developed to habitually prevent the free expression of a nuclear emotional conflict in the individual.

He places great emphasis on the dynamic relationship between head, neck, and torso as the "primary control" for the pattern of tension displayed by the rest of the body. Viewing this area as the site for mechanisms which orient the person in space (e.g., balance, vision, etc.), Alexander maintained that relief of tension patterns in this area had profound effects on one's relationship with the outer world.

The movement reeducation program, which also focuses on the pattern of breathing movements, seeks to replace old patterns with improved ones. This is accomplished when the head moves *up* from the top of the spine, the spine lengthens, and abnormal curves and pressures are relieved. An elevation of mood and improvement of one's self-esteem is believed to follow on the heels of improvement in physical competence.[19]

There are basic differences among these various approaches to healing in terms of emphasis; greater awareness of lived-body, removing chronic tension and pain, inducing states of relaxed awareness, realigning the body, and so on. And yet, they share many basic similarities — chief of which is the intention to free and harmonize the flow of life-energy with the direction and flow of our movement as unique individuals. Perhaps a deeper significance is captured in the meanings of the morphemes in the word AIKIDO: "AI" as uniting or bringing together, "KI" the life energy or spirit, and "DO" — to the path, the way.[20]

Notes

1. Zinker, Joseph C. Introduction, In *Body Process: A Gestalt Approach to Working with the Body in Psychotherapy* by James I. Kepner, 1987, Gestalt Institute of Cleveland Press, Cleveland.

2. Tulku, Tarthang. *Kum Nye Relaxation: Theory, Preparation, Massage*, 1978, Dharma Publishing, Berkeley.

3. Chaitow, Leon. *The Acupuncture Treatment of Pain*, 1977, Arco Publishing, New York.

4. Ebner, Maria. *Connective Tissue Massage: Theory and Therapeutic Application*, 1975, Robert E. Krieger Publishing Co., Huntington, New York.

5. Beck, Mark. *The Theory and Practice of Therapeutic Massage*, 1988, Milady Publishing/Wiley, New York.

6. Luce, Gay Gaer. *Body Time*, 1971, Pantheon Books, New York.

7. Stone, Randolph. *Energy: The Vital Polarity in the Healing Arts*, 1957, 7557 Merrill Avenue, Chicago.

8. Rolf, Ida. *Rolfing: The Integration of Human Structures*, 1977, Harper and Row, New York.

9. Hirai, Tomio. *Zen Meditation Therapy*, 1975, Japan Publications, Tokyo.

10. Reynolds, David K. *The Quiet Therapies: Japanese Pathways to Personal Growth*, 1980, University Press of Hawaii, Honolulu.

11. Wallace, R. K. and H. Benson. The Physiology of Meditation, 1972, *Scientific American*, 227, 84–90.

12. Goldstein, Joseph. *The Experience of Insight*, 1983, Shambhala, Boston.

13. Feuerstein, Georg. *The Essence of Yoga*, 1974, Grove Press, New York.

14. Wickramasekera, I., ed. *Biofeedback, Behavior Therapy and Hypnosis*, 1976, Nelson-Hall, Chicago.

15. Feldenkrais, Moshe. *Awareness Through Movement*, 1972, Harper and Row, New York.

16. Bennett, H. Behavioral Anesthesia, *Advances*, 1985, 2 (4), 11–21.

17. DeRopp, R. S. *The Master Game*, 1968, Delta, New York.

18. Doleys, Daniel M., R. L. Meredith, and A. R. Ciminero. *Behavioral Medicine: Assessment and Treatment Strategies*, 1982, Plenum Press, New York.

19. Ottiwell, Frank. The Alexander Technique, in *Your Body Works*, Gerald Kagan, ed., 1981, And/Or Press, Berkeley.

20. Leonard, George. Aikido and the Mind of the West, *Intellectual Digest*, June, 1973.

Suggested Readings

Alexander, F. M. *The Use of Self*, 1938, Methuen and Co., Ltd., London.

Arya, U. *Meditation and the Art of Dying*, 1979, Himalayan International Institute, Honedale, PA.

Fischer, R. A cartography of ecstatic and meditative states, *Science*, 1971, 174, 897–904.

Jacobsen, E. *Progressive Relaxation*, 1929, University of Chicago Press, Chicago.

LeShan, Lawrence. *How to Meditate*, 1975, Bantam Books, New York.

Tart, Charles. *Waking Up: Overcoming the Obstacles to Human Potential*, 1986, New Science Library/Shambhala, Boston.

Part Two
Framework

7

Love, Knowledge, and the Body/Mind Paradigm

Two Einsteins are on a beach, one is scribbling formulas,
the other is playing the violin —
the paradoxes of science and art,
reason and intuition,
numbers and notes,
measurement and judgement,
physics and mysticism,
time and death.
Would it be too far-fetched to invoke the
Einsteinian universe,
a cosmos neither measureable
nor infinite, but curving back upon itself,
curving back and becoming itself again —
a universe at once self-contained
yet endless in variety, like the eight notes of a scale?
And the beach, like Einstein,
less a symbol than a kind of effigy —
suggesting finally not a world of paradox
but of the meeting of polarities
                    —author unknown, *Einstein on the Beach*

The field of psychology was founded upon the scientific model of classical physics. This model holds that the world, and everything in it, is composed of particles (atoms, molecules, cells, etc.) which are structured and function according to certain laws of nature. And, accordingly, when these scientific laws are all discovered and fully applied, humankind will achieve complete prediction, control and scientific understanding of the material world, including itself.

It isn't working out according to plan, however! Beginning with Einstein's theories, a new model, based on quantum physics, has taken hold which is based on the principle that all matter in the universe, human and otherwise, is, at one and the same time, highly ordered and highly random, sometimes as particles, sometimes as waves. In this

sense, the model originally adopted by psychology as its own is becoming an outmoded relic.

"Quantum physics," according to physicist Fred Alan Wolf,[1] "has
provided a new vision of the construction of the universe and every mi-
croscopic part that it contains. This includes, of course, the brain that
is conceiving and directing the traffic of neural flow in forming the very
words that I'm speaking. Processes within the brain must follow the
law of quantum physics if they follow any physical principles at all.
These laws are as different from the deterministic laws of classical
mechanics as a time-machine is to a horse-drawn carriage."

Neuroscientists, such as Richard Restak[2], point out that along
with all other matter in the universe, the human nervous system is a
highly ordered structure *and* a highly randomized structure, at one
and the same time. Recordings of brain activity, for example, display
key patterns that are alike from one person to another — although no
two EEG patterns are precisely the same, including those taken from
the same person. Correspondingly, recordings of electrical activity in
individual neurons exhibit a randomness and spontaneity of firing that
make it simply impossible to predict the behavior of a particular nerve
cell with any precision, at any particular point in time.

In many ways, the human brain conforms to the model of classical physics, and, in other ways, to the model of quantum physics. In
this sense, the brain reveals a complementarity of structure and function: on the one hand, it is highly specific and localized — if you dis-
turb one part of it, specific functions will be lost. On the other hand,
the human brain functions holistically — if one part of it is damaged or
disturbed, another part may very well take its place.

Stanford neurosurgeon Karl Pribram[3] states, "Removing a hunk
of brain or injuring one or another portion of the brain does not excise
a particular memory or set of memories. The process of remembering
may be disturbed in some general way, or even some aspect of the general process may be disrupted. But never is a single memory trace of
some particular experience lost while all else that is memorable is re-
tained. Thus in some way or other memory must become distributed
... over a sufficient expanse of brain to make the memory of that experience resistant to brain damage."

The localized and holistic aspects of the human brain are complementary — not contradictory. Is light a wave or a particle? Physi-
cists have discovered that it is actually *both*, depending on the instruments used to measure it. Similarly, whether the brain appears as
holistic or localized also depends on the way experiments are de-
signed to study the question. Whether in physics or psychology, the ob-

server is inseparable from the observations made, the questions asked, the experimental designs employed, and the instruments used to probe for answers.

In his book, *Taking the Quantum Leap*, Wolf concludes that, "The world exists in two complementary guises. Each guise complements the other in the sense that you cannot experience one guise while you are experiencing the other." In other words, the world of our unique inner experience partakes of, and is at one with, the complementarity we share with the neurons, molecules and subatomic particles that make us up.

Is light a wave or a particle? Is the real world predictable or chaotic? Are we separate or are we whole? In any given moment of our lives, an array of possible courses of action is available to us which appears as infinite in number. And yet, at a certain juncture, in a special moment, we choose one particular path among the many and, in that split second, the world of infinite possibilities collapses into *one*. At that point of intending, of choosing, all other possibilities disappear, completely — or endure, at most, as apologies and regrets for actions delayed, avoided or not taken.

Our intention to act, then, alters the probability that one neuron will release a minute quantum of chemicals that will spark across the synaptic gap to stimulate a second neuron into action. If enough chemicals are released in unison, only then will there be sufficient chemical transmitters to fire the second neuron. Our act of intention and choice, and the "firing" of that second neuron are, thus, one and the same — complementary aspects of the same phenomenon. In the act of intending, of choosing, and of moving along a uniquely chosen path, the quantum world of infinite possibilities is transformed, instantly, into one unique experiential world — created by each of us, in each and every moment.

Often, we seem to inhabit a fractured, split-level, and ruptured world where the seemingly separate realms of feeling and thought, body and mind, are rarely in balance. Too much prediction, control and rigidity in our thinking — an obsession with future scenarios, for instance — finds us in a world empty of pleasure, joy and an embodied sense of self. On the other hand, too much immersion in feelings and emotions — self-indulgence, for instance, finds us in a world devoid of values, ethics and meaning. The principle of complementarity embodied in the new quantum physics offers Body/Mind Psychology a new model, and language, with which we might begin to put these fractured concepts and existential dilemmas into a dynamic, unified body-of-knowledge.

The Body/Mind Paradigm

A paradigm is simply a collection of ideas, insights and facts which, when taken together, form a meaningful pattern or *gestalt.*

It may seem somewhat strange that an emerging movement in the field of psychology would choose a term like body/mind to identify its paradigm and to convey meaning to others. After all, wouldn't a term like *bodymind* or *mindbody* better convey the intended meaning that body and mind are assumed to be one and the same in nature and unitary in function?

The simple answer has to do with use of the slash or virgule (/) in the word body/mind — and the distinctions it provides:

> **vir-gule,** *n.* L *virgula,* 1. a short oblique stroke (/) between two words indicating that whichever is appropriate may be chosen to complete the sense of the text in which they occur.
> (*The Random House Dictionary,* Unabridged Edition)

When we use the virgule in the term "miles/gallon," it is clear in terms of what we are actually trying to calculate and communicate, that the word on one side of the virgule is meaningless without the word on the other side. If we are interested in knowing something about the fuel consumption of an automobile, it would be useless to know how many miles it travelled without knowing how many gallons of fuel it consumed — and vice versa.

Similarly, in using the term body/mind, we are asserting that any attempt to calculate or understand the world of human experience or behavior has no meaning without including the processes of *both* body and mind in their interrelationship.

And yet, there is real hesitancy to phrase body/mind as a relationship. To say there is something *here* that is related to something *there*, while both are one and the same, seems irrational. However, in observing the natural world, we constantly see opposites comprising actions, conditions and events. There is an up and a down and they are both parts of the concept of "verticality." Without both terms, *in relationship*, the concept of verticality would be meaningless. Similarly, there would be no meaning to the word happiness without the idea of unhappiness. In fact, without these polar opposites in language, there would be no meaningful language. So, the virgule in the term body/mind is meant to convey that although each pole has its functions and separate identity *in language,* it is misleading to assume that "body" and "mind" are in any way separate or limited in terms of psychological processes. This definition is synonymous with the Japanese concept of *shin shin*—the identity of body and mind interpreted as originally one and the same.[4]

Any paradigm attempts aiming an observer in a particular direction, as well as providing clues to the solution to certain problems. Adherents to the body/mind paradigm have chosen this particular term because, while allowing for the full use of language in synthesizing and communicating ideas, the term also provides a warning to us not to become sidetracked by placing artificial limitations on our theoretical and practical explorations.

We have treated body and mind as separate entities and separate realms of study for centuries. Now an alternative is opening up to us—an *identity hypothesis* — which holds that, above and beyond mere correlation or causality, two events are identical if they occur in the same place at the same time. We can observe this synchronicity between bodily processes, emotional states, and mental events in time and space. There is strong coincidence between simultaneous events of similar duration as they occur, say, in the brain and our musculature and our conscious experience.

This identity hypothesis, although hardly solving the centuries old body/mind riddle, at least allows us to put it aside temporarily in favor of a working model — which is what experimental researchers have always done anyway!

Love Knowledge and Methodology

Just as Heisenberg[5] discovered within the science of physics, proponents of a body/mind psychology have come to the conclusion that as we probe deeper and deeper into the world of human experience, the same paradox emerges.

Encapsulation in a purely rational-empirical way of knowing has produced a psychology cocooned in a purely objective methodology—a kind of *post reductio absurdum*.

This model never recognizes the unitary nature of observation. Instead, it rests on the object-subject dichotomy:

"I AM SUBJECT"   (PSYCHOLOGIST)
"YOU ARE OBJECT"   (OTHER)

This traditional method of studying human experience and behavior has provided many advantages — along with strangling limitations. These limitations grow from a paradox and the paradox is this:

At the subtlest levels on which objective science operates, objectivity
becomes impossible because the very act of observing changes the situation observed.

Whether a physicist studying the behavior of subatomic particles,
or an anthropologist studying the customs of a small tribe, the presence of the observer, or the observing instruments, alters the situation
beyond our ability to account for it. *Subjectivity intrudes.* The observer and the observed merge, person and environment become
united. Since there are no limits to what constitutes your or my environment (except for arbitrary ones), our own superstructure of beliefs
and attitudes influences what we perceive — no matter how deep our
commitment to observe objectively.

As long as we, as psychologists, continue to separate ourselves
from our subjects as purely "other things," we will continue to suffer
from a poverty of relevent theory, research and healing practices —
and remain cocooned in a cultural mind-set that supports deperson-
alization and dehumanization. To objectify other persons in an effort
to understand human experience is analogous to freezing rivers in an
effort to understand their flow.

Almost in reaction to this objectification of human behavior and
experience, some vanguard body/mind researchers tried to develop a
methodology based on the statement:

"I AM SUBJECT"   (PSYCHOLOGIST)
"YOU ARE SUBJECT"   (OTHER PERSON)

This position attempted to explore the possibility of understanding human experience in terms of purely subjective knowledge: "If I,
as psychologist, can access my own feelings, intuitions and thoughts,
then I can come to empathize with your experience to the extent that
we share a common experiential world."

We can all agree, however, that I can't experience your experiential world, directly — nor can you experience mine. In fact, it appears
to be just as limiting to say that one can only form insights about another's experience by observing one's own; as it is to say that one can
only form insights by objectifying the other person and detaching from
one's own experience. As Mandler and Mandler[6] make so clear, the
method of "subjectification" was, in retrospect, an emerging psychology's attempt at grabbing on to one horn of a dualistic dilemma in its
attempt to free itself from the other.

A methodology based on subjectivity limits us in even the simplest of situations. For instance, if you are color blind while I am not,

how am I to empathize with your experience of the natural world. The point, of course, is that I cannot, precisely.

Abraham Maslow[7] proposed a middle path to resolving this sub-ject-object dichotomy — which he termed *taoistic objectivity* or *love knowledge*. This methodology is based on a distinction between view-ing *other* as a moral object — as opposed to *other* as epistemological object. When we separate subject from object for various scientific or moralistic purposes, we meet the criteria of classical objectivity, and fall into the old trap of viewing person-as-thing. However, if we sepa-rate subject from object for the purpose of understanding, and even-tually, for the purpose of surmounting our separation through recog-nition of both our commonalities and individual uniqueness, we complement *classical objectivity* with love knowledge.

If you, my color-blind friend, are celebrating a birthday and I choose to buy you a gallery poster as a gift, I can, of course, just take my chances. On the other hand, I can approach you as a taoistic object of wonder and curiosity — and choose to study the transformations that take place between your private experience of visual events (which I cannot know, directly) and the verbal/body language you use to express those experiences (which I can know, directly). I choose this peaceful graphic in pastels, I hand it to you, you remain expres-sionless and then say "It's bland." I say this other combination of shapes and colors is offensive, you say they are exciting. I am not able to understand the basis upon which you make these judgements, but I may, over time, come to a determination of what you find to be beau-tiful, and choose just the right birthday gift for you. By the act of sus-pending my own presuppositions about the structure of your experi-ence, and in treating you as taoistic object, I have come to better understand you as a subject, as a person.

Taoistic Objectivity is to Western consciousness what zen or vi-passana is to Eastern consciousness — it is an attitude toward know-ing and insight which recognizes the loving-perception in parent-child relationships, between lovers, between good friends. Such an attitude produces an interest and fascination on the part of the "observer," and an openness—a dropping of defenses—on the part of the subject. The parents, fascinated with their newborn; the lovers, intent on exploring each other, let themselves be enervated by their inter-curiosity.

Love relationships provide a ground where we each become fath-omable. If we love, are attracted to, fascinated by, or profoundly inter-ested in another, we are less tempted to control them, change them, im-prove them or interfere with their unfolding process. Alternately, according to Maslow, in the act of prizing other, we are more apt to recognize our connectedness to them—and to use that connectedness as a vehicle to explore deeper and more relevant insights into the psychological architecture of their world. In a real sense, Maslow muses, love knowledge may be more accurate, more true.

Taoistic Objectivity is integral to forming the general framework of a Body/Mind Psychology — in terms of its theory construction, research methodology, and healing practices. Just as the term body/mind speaks to the inclusion and integration of what were previously separate and distinct *realms* of study, taoistic objectivity acknowledges the inclusion and integration of what were previously separate and distinct *methods* of study.

However, Maslow cautions us, just as pure objectivity and pure subjectivity can produce certain blindness, so too can taoistic objectivity. The same love, fascination and interest which is a vehicle for understanding self and others, can, in another situation, produce a form of absorption and immersion which distorts perception so that other paths to knowledge remain hidden.

Taoistic objectivity is a beginning rather than an end in itself. It is an umbrella beneath which various paths to truth might both maintain their distinctions, as well as merge and criss-cross, like tracks on a sandy beach, into even newer pathways to understanding. In the words of Atisha, ancient Buddhist scholar, "Since wisdom without method and method without wisdom have been termed 'bondage,' one should never discard either of them."[8]

Notes

1. Wolf, Fred Alan. *Taking the Quantum Leap,* 1981, Harper and Row, New York.

2. Restak, Richard. *The Infant Brain,* 1986, Doubleday, New York.

3. Pribram, Karl. What the Fuss Is All About, In *The Holographic Paradigm and Other Paradoxes,* Ken Wilber, ed., 1982, New Science Library/Shambhala, Boston.

4. Shaner, David Edward. *The Bodymind Experience in Japanese Buddhism,* 1985, SUNY Press, Albany, New York.

5. Heisenberg, W. *Physical Principles of the Quantum Theory,* 1930, New York.

6. Mandler, Jean and George Mandler. The Subject-Object Dichotomy, *Journal of Humanistic Psychology,* 14 (4), Fall, 1974.

7. Maslow, Abraham. *The Farther Reaches of Human Nature*, 1971, Viking Press, New York.

8. Batchelor, Stephen. *Alone With Others: An Existential Approach to Buddhism*, 1983, Grove Press, New York, p. 90.

Suggested Readings

Comfort, Alex. *Reality and Empathy*, 1984, SUNY Press, Albany, New York.

Harman, Willis. *Global Mind Change*, 1988, Knowledge Systems, Inc., Indianapolis, Indiana.

Maslow, Abraham. *Toward a Psychology of Being*, 1962, Van Nostrand, New York.

Pribram, Karl. *Languages of the Brain: Experimental Paradoxes and Principles in Neuropsychology*, 1971, Brandon House, New York.

Sacks, Oliver, *The Man Who Mistook His Wife for a Hat and Other Clinical Tales*, 1985, Summit Books, New York.

8

The Holographic Model

If the brain is a hologram interpreting a holographic universe, the possibility exists for the interface of personal and transpersonal consciousness. Such a contact may constitute the 'right seeing' or enlightenment, spoken of by mystics. Obviously such a state is highly prized and goes beyond most expectations for conventional psychotherapy.[1]

In the history of ideas, it has been useful to engage the most recent invention as a model to describe how the human body works. During the Greek epoch, when water ducts came into use, the idea took hold that the body was a series of ducts carrying powerful bodily fluids which controlled our thoughts, moods, emotions, and so on. Later, when pumps came into use, they too became the working model to describe the inner workings of the body.

With the Industrial Revolution, the human organism was viewed as a composite of interlocking parts which functioned like a well-tuned machine. The telegraph and the telephone also enjoyed their day in the spotlight. And today, with the advancement of the computer age, the idea that the nervous system functions like a state-of-the-art computer is very much in vogue.

Be they ducts, pumps, machines, clocks, telephones or high-tech computers, however, all share a similar principle — of parts stacking together to form a mechanism.

These *mechanomorphic* models — of human beings as machines — have allowed us to greatly expand our body-of-knowledge. But as much as they aid us in our understanding, they also force us to discard concern for any human issue or process which doesn't fit the classical model. These are the so called *ghosts* in the machine: the unconscious, self-awareness, creativity, love, violence, madness, and vast realms of human experience. When applied to the world of human experience, the machine-based models consistently fail to account for our uniqueness and integrity as individuals. They have, naturally, disappointed us because although they may excel in the analytic study of things and productions, they offer little that is helpful to the study of uniquely human processes.

The computer model, for instance, when it offers us something more than wondrous calculators, can point to the field of *artificial intelligence* and its many breakthroughs in simulating human thinking. But these grandest of computers do not feel, they can't emote, or dream or create self-quests for meaning and authenticity. The robot machines never do fully move like you and me, and even the most advanced computer doesn't approach the intelligence, the creativity, or the capacity for love and passion manifest in a single human being.

In each and every case, these attempts at envisioning the human being as machine-like in make-up seem to supply about half of the pieces to the human puzzle. Although deeply useful, they come up short — as indeed they must — because they can only compute that which is equal to the sum of their parts, never more.

A Body/Mind Psychology, if it is to thrive in terms of theory, research, and application, must adopt a working model of an entirely different sort, namely, one which allows for reconstructions that are *more than the sum of parts*. How else are we to come to grips with the human unconscious, with human creativity, and the madness and violence in our midst.

The holograph provides just such a working model — and one which offers an astoundingly new way of envisioning body/mind, and perhaps, the human spirit as well. As Karl Pribram[2] notes, "until recently, brain and behavioral scientists could not conceive of any mechanism that was consonant with the facts of brain anatomy and physiology and at the same time spread sensory input sufficiently to account for the distributed memory store. Now a plausible mechanism has been discovered."

We are not addressing some fancy new gadget here. The holograph, in a very real sense, throws open the limits to what we can know; and offers the possibility of expanding our body-of-knowledge into domains never before imagined.

The holographic model operates on principles which force a reversal in our usual ways of thinking. Unlike the machine models, in which we attempt to solve puzzles based on how the parts stack together to form the whole—holography provides a model in which *each and every part embodies and contains the whole*.

Outer World/Inner World

A hologram is created by the intersecting beams of laser light — a very pure form of light.[3] The beam of light emanating from the laser is split to create two beams, one of which shines on an object and the other, termed the reference beam, directly impacts a photographic plate.

Like waves converging on a beach, the two beams interfere with each other to create new wave patterns. Where the crests and troughs of the two beams reinforce each other, stronger waves are created. Where the troughs and crests are out of phase, they cancel each other out. The resulting interference pattern is recorded on the photographic plate. When the film is developed, it becomes a permanent, three-dimensional record of the infinitely complex wave patterns. (An interference pattern can be created by bringing the pads of the thumb and index fingers slowly together, and then apart, about two inches in front of one opened eye.)

Illuminated by a laser beam, the hologram diffracts and bends the light to re-create a three-dimensional image of the original object. As the light spreads out, viewers in different locations perceive the waves exactly as they were reflected from the original object—creating the full image of the object, suspended in three-dimensional space.

If we return to the photographic plate for a moment, we discover something quite astounding. We find that light waves from every spot on the original object, interacting with the reference beam, are recorded *everywhere*. If a part of the plate, any sized part, is broken off from the whole and illuminated with the appropriate wave-length of laser light, the full image of the original object is created *in its entirety*. It is this unique way of storing information which is the most fascinating property of the holograph and which offers the most fascinating implications as to how body/mind creates the world of human experience.

A more familiar feature of the holograph is that countless images may be stacked onto a single plate by using different wave-lengths of laser light to record each one. In this way, each wave-length is capable of retrieving its own separate image while remaining merely a part of the many separate images composing the holographic plate.

Holography combines these two unique information storage-and-retrieval systems in the same unit. In the more familiar system, the sum of the parts is equal to the whole; the plate is composed of the many images recorded upon it. In the new system, the whole is contained in each of the parts; each part of each hologram contains the whole image.

To Body/Mind Psychology, the implications of the first, more familiar system, that the sum of the parts is equal to the whole, offers little that is new. Here we are referring to the external order of things — measurable things. I am a configuration of atoms, molecules, cells and organs which make me up. I am part of a family, in a particular geographic region, in a particular country, on a particular planet in a particular solar system and so on. This information system serves the human experience of the differentiation of discrete and separate things. It is based on our capacity to scan the environment in a sequential manner — filtering data relevant to satisfying our own needs and wants. This is the stuff of thought, rationality, concepts, strategies, spread-sheets, and the scientific world-view. This is the system that has defined the boundaries of our Western body-of-knowledge for centuries.

Turn to the newly discovered system, however, and an entirely unique domain opens before us — one from which we might begin to make sense of the interior world of human images and ideas: archetypal and personal unconscious; spiritual experiences; the distorted stuff of dreams and nightmares; and the basis for our Eastern body-of-knowledge.

The principles of holography begin to suggest how a mental image or feeling state can be the same as a discharge of neurons; and how the tiniest component of a memory engram can conjure the whole of the memory.

From the simplest body sensation, say the smell of freshly baked bread, to our more archetypal imaginings, in which the boundary between self and world dissolves into an undifferentiated oneness — human mysteries become accessible to our understanding. Speculations, based on this new information system, suggest that each of us, like some unique part of a grander hologram, is composed of countless holograms — each embodying personal and transpersonal memories buried within each organ, muscle, cell, molecule; species, tribe and nation.

Body Holograms/Phantom Limbs

A glimpse into the holography of the body/mind experience is provided by research into the experience of the "phantom limb."

The phenomenon of the phantom limb has mystified physicians, nurses, and research psychologists for decades. M. L. Simmel,[4] a clinical researcher who has studied the phantom limb mystery for decades offers this summary description:

> Immediately after the amputation, as he awakes from the anesthesia, the patient may not believe that the limb has been removed until he can convince himself by looking under the covers.

But even once he knows beyond doubt that the extremity is gone, he typically continues to feel it as if it were still present. In the days — and years — to come, the foot of the amputated leg may itch; as the patient reaches down to scratch it, he reaches for an empty space. He may feel the bedsheets on the arm or leg; he may feel a mild, perhaps, pleasant, tingling; or much more rarely, he may feel pain. He may feel that he can wiggle his fingers or toes, flex or extend the wrist or ankle, and that he can perform these movements more or less at will. Despite his knowledge that the amputation has been performed, the patient may 'forget' and reach out with the missing hand to grasp something, or to steady himself, or he may step on the phantom foot and fall.

These phantom limb phenomena may offer some clues as to how body and mind are unified, holographically, to form our very sense-of-self. For instance, if a deformed limb has been amputated, the phantom limb will likewise be experienced as deformed in the body/mind experience of the amputee. However, this is the case only if the deformed limb participated in the patient's ongoing experience. The loss of a nonfunctional limb does not result in the phantom limb experience.

Simmel also reports that the age at which the limb loss occurs effects the likelihood of experiencing the phantom limb. If the amputation occurred before four years of age, only 23 percent of amputees reported phantoms. If limb loss occurred after eight years of age, 100 percent reported the phantom limb experience. Interestingly, in the case of leprosy patients, where limb loss is gradual and undramatic, taking ten years or more, there are no reports of phantom limbs.

Phantom limb phenomena suggest that the human body cannot be an object like any other thing with definite boundaries and shape. Holographically, like conscious experience itself, the body is not simply a physical form extending from the crown of the head to the soles of the feet. Rather, the body is functionally identical with our uniquely experienced sense-of-self — changing and ever redefining, but always configured holistically.

From this perspective, the "first-order"[5] body/mind experience may be seen as the fundamental ground — the seamless horizon — from which all our discrete experiences take form. Our unique capacity for self-reflection, like waves of laser light, is capable of passing through and illuminating the countless holograms which make-up our sense-of-self. The light of consciousness—bent, refracted and reflected in various states, is, perhaps, the same source of spiritual illumination of which mystics have spoken throughout the ages.[6]

As a working model for a Body/Mind Psychology, the holograph offers us a vista from which we may begin to envision a middle ground of unity between seemingly inseparable opposites. This is a ground of synthesis—between physical and virtual; between outer world and inner world; between body/mind and spirit.

Notes

1. Osborne, G. and D. Baldwin. Psychotherapy: From One State of Illusion to Another, *Psychotherapy Theory, Research and Practice*, 1982, Fall, 19 (3), 266–75.

2. Pribram, Karl. What the Fuss is All About. In *The Holographic Paradigm and Other Paradoxes*, Ken Wilber, ed., 1982, New Science Library/Shambhala, Boston.

3. Boraiko, Allen A. Lasers: A Splendid Light, *National Geographic*, March, 1984, 165 (3).

4. Simmel, M. L. The Body Percept in Physical Medicine and Rehabilitation. *Journal of Health and Social Behavior*, 1967, 8, 60–64.

5. Shaner, David Edward. *The Bodymind Experience in Japanese Buddhism*, 1986, SUNY Press, Albany, New York.

6. Mann, Richard. *The Light of Consciousness*, 1984, SUNY Press, Albany, New York.

Suggested Readings

Globus, G., G. Maxwell and I. Savodnik, eds. *Consciousness and the Brain: A Scientific and Philosophical Inquiry*, 1976, Plenum, New York.

Hadley, June. The Representational System: A Bridging Concept for Psychoanalysis and Neurophysiology, *International Review of Psychoanalysis*, 1983, 10 (1), 13–30.

Penrose, Roger. *The Emperor's New Mind: Concerning Computers, Minds, and the Laws of Physics*, 1990, Oxford University Press, New York.

Pollio, Howard R. *Behavior and Existence*, 1982, Brooks/Cole, Monterey, California.

Pribram, Karl. Behaviorism, Phenomenology and Holism in Psychology: A Scientific Analysis, *Journal of Social and Biological Structure*, 1979, 2, 65–72.

Roszak, Theodore, *The Cult of Information: The Folklore of Computers and the True Art of Thinking*, 1986, Pantheon, New York.

Tart, Charles T., ed. *Altered States of Consciousness: A Book of Readings, 1969, John Wiley and Sons, Inc., New York.*

Wolman, B. and M. Ullman, eds. Handbook of Altered States of Consciousness, 1975, Van Nostrand, New York.

Zinkin, L. The Hologram as a Model for Analytical Psychology, *Journal of Analytical Psychology*, 1987, 32, 1–21.

9

The Healing Model

You can hold yourself back from the sufferings of the world, this is something you are to do and is in accord with your nature, but precisely this
holding back is the only suffering that you might be able to avoid.
                                                                    — Franz Kafka

Life is, fundamentally *movement*. A rock is stagnant, unmoving.
It is victim to the water which eventually dissolves it; the air which bat-
ters its form; and, ultimately, its very existence. The *living*, however,
experience a continuing, alternating rhythm of contraction and expansion which gives form to our entire being. Our cells expand and contract, our muscles stretch and contract — our hearts can be open or
closed.[1]

In the broadest sense, the power of living organisms to *move* is
our most striking characteristic. In evolution, as organisms develop
more and more complex nervous systems, they claim more and more
varieties of movement into their lives. From reptiles, to mammals, to
human beings, the evolving brain permits for an ever-expanding range
of interactions — and subtleties of movement.

Brain Storms

Sitting directly atop of our spinal cords is the oldest part of the
human brain, the hindbrain. First seen in its entirety in reptiles, this
reptilian brain works to meet our grossest survival needs. It is concerned with our physical movement in the environment; with eating,
drinking, temperature control, fight-flight responses; cycles of sleep and
wakefulness; and, the mechanics of sexuality. It is the *id*-brain — the
reflexive, pleasure-seeking, pain-avoiding brain which deals with the
world in two primal ways: *approach* or *avoid, fight* or *flee*.

Layered above the reptilian brain is the mid-brain—which is first
seen, in its entirety, in higher mammals. Unlike the reflexive, hard-wired
reptilian brain, the *mammalian brain* opens to the world of *emotion*;

to fear, pleasure, surprise, boredom, curiosity, affection, sadness, play-
fulness, rage, disgust, anxiety, and a host of other emotional states.
The word emotion, itself, derives from the Latin *e* (out) and *movere* (to
move): to move outward. This more subtle mammalian brain, the *ego-*
brain, adds a period of delay between a perception and an action
which provides for an evaluation of an event based on our subjective
experience of the pleasantness or unpleasantness of our accompanying emotional state.

The third brain, or forebrain, is first seen in its entirety in human
beings. It is composed of a mushroom-like mantle of convoluted tissue
surrounding the two older brains below it. This is the language brain,
the self-reflecting *superego*-brain, and, it is the most fundamental characteristic of our species.

This layer of *human brain* involves itself with what are truly
evolutionary novelties for our species, namely, *language* and *self-*
awareness.

From our uniquely human brain emerges both the world of self-
awareness, and the ability to construct *holographic*/language models
of that world based on past memories, present experience, and anticipated futures. Once constructed, the human brain allows for *self* to
make "trial" movements inside these holograms through the processes
of cognition, imagination, dreaming and other states of consciousness.
The human brain creates an expanded period of delay between perception and action in which to search our memories, and, evaluate the
emotional effects of anticipated actions on present as well as future
scenarios.

Each brain-layer responds with movement that begins with some
tension-pattern within us. The tension may originate as a purely physical imbalance, such as hunger for food; or as conflicted emotional
expression; or as the cognitive dysfunction and worry experienced in
the confusion of our emotions, thoughts, and actions. Wherever a tension pattern originates, our attempt is always to relieve the tension by
completion of some form of movement.

The three-brain theory was first proposed by neurologist Paul
MacLean,[2] chief researcher at the National Institute for Mental Health
in Washington, D.C. Based on decades of brain research, he has concluded that due to ruinous errors in brain design, there is, often, in-
sufficient communication and coordination between the three strata
of brain.

This lack of communication results in an ongoing dissociation
between the higher and lower brains which is experienced within us,
and between us, as conflicted emotions and actions, unconscious

and conscious, savage and sane, rational and irrational, and so on. MacLean terms this ongoing conflict between the reptilian, mammalian and human layers of brain, *schizophysiology*.

Schizophysiology and the Emotions

> When you hear the word, you will *feel* this way — experience this state of mind strongly. You will show it in your outward behavior in a natural manner. You may do anything you like ... anything at all. You will not be annoyed or embarrassed by our presence in the room. Afterward, you will be able to describe what happened.

Thus began the instructions to hypnotized subjects in a series of studies by Nina Bull[3] which stand as classics in the field of body/mind research because of the many insights they provide into the origins of schizophysiology and psychiatric disorder.

Once induced into hypnotic trance and given the above instructions, researchers slowly counted to five and pronounced one of six words: *fear, anger, disgust, depression, joy,* and *triumph.* The actions of each subject were recorded for each of the conditions, and when the emotion had run its course, each participant was asked to verbally describe the experience. In this way, Bull and her collaborators, at Columbia University, began their ingenious explorations of the psychosomatic bridge which connects our emotional and mental life to the life of the body.

By analyzing bodily patterns of movement and correlating them with each subject's firsthand report of the emotional experience, researchers arrived at a number of fascinating discoveries. For instance, records revealed that when we experience emotions which are considered unpleasant, such as fear, anger, and disgust, our bodily movement always involves some basic form of conflict and frustration. In fear, for instance, this conflict might best be described as moving to escape, while at the same time, being frozen to the spot. Certain muscle groups controlling our postural responses freeze in contraction, while opposing muscles tense in readiness for escape from the feared situation.

In disgust, the conflict is between postural movement which readies us to turn away, while the opposing visceral response is to nausea and muscular preparation for vomiting.

In anger, Bull interpreted the conflict as between a forward-moving attack response involving hands, arms, and voice, and an opposing muscular pattern meant to restrain and control — keeping hands, arms, and vocal response suspended.

Bull concluded that in all three "primitive emotions," fear, anger and disgust, there is a common pattern in which a primary muscular movement is repressed or blocked by a secondary movement directed at restraining the impulse to act. This basic bodily conflict determines what we subjectively experience as unpleasant in fear, anger, and disgust.

In depression, Bull discovered that a complex pattern of blocked movements is created which reflects a combination of fear, anger, and disgust — but turned inward on oneself and experienced as sadness and depression.

Subjects experiencing depression assumed a slumping posture, with a long, heavy facial expression as might be seen in a sulking child. Subjects reported a strong pressure in the chest, difficulty in breathing, a slowing down of movement, and feelings of weakness and lethargy. Their verbal reports supported the finding that depression is actually a succession of fear, anger, and disgust in various sequences. Subjects reported a desire to cry with a sorry feeling, not caring, feeling angry — followed by feelings of guilt and self-disgust at being angry — and fear that nothing would ever change in life. All participants appeared to share the perception of some interference with the act of *moving*, combined with an overriding sense of frustration.

In joy and triumph, on the other hand, a pattern of responses was observed which was a complete reversal of those recorded in the emotions of fear, anger, disgust, and depression. In each case, upon hearing the pronouncement "joy" or "triumph," the person straightened up, smiled or laughed, with the face becoming broad and wide. Breathing was deeper and freer, bodily movement increased, and pleasant feelings of being energized and enabled were reported. Bull states, "It was as though frustration was completely done away with and a positive orientation established. ... "

Frozen Bodies

In the first series of experiments, Bull and associates discovered that our basic linkage to our emotional life is through various patterns of bodily movement, some pleasantly synchronous, others unpleasantly conflicted.

In a second series of experiments, these researchers went further in bridging our understanding of the body/mind connection. These studies involved the same hypnotic induction as was used in the first experiments, but this time, participants were asked to "lock" their bodies into the bodily pattern described by the researcher—muscular patterns corresponded to each of the six emotional states. It was found that each participant reported subjective emotional states which corresponded to the muscular pattern in which they had "frozen" their bodies. For example, a person asked to tighten the visceral muscles, while twisting the body, reported feeling "disgusted." Those subjects with bodies locked in fear, reported feeling "fearful." In other sessions, while assuming the movement pattern connected with joy, individuals reported feeling "joyful."

In a further step, however, these researchers discovered that when subjects were frozen in a specific muscular pattern, they could *not* experience any other emotional state. A person locked into the posture corresponding to, say, fear, found it impossible to feel joy, anger, or any other emotional state suggested by the researcher — until given permission to "unlock" the fear pattern and move to the new pattern.

With far-reaching implications for a Body/Mind Psychology, these researchers discovered that if our bodies are muscularly frozen in a particular emotional pattern, we remain predisposed to experience only those feelings connected with that emotion — finding it difficult, if not impossible, to fully experience any other emotional state until the body is unlocked and permitted to freely move once again.

Bull's discovery that depression is experienced as lethargy, fatigue, and resistance to movement suggests a system that has broken down under the stress born of repressing various primitive emotions. This breakdown is cognitively reflected in thought-patterns which are self-negating, anxious, hopeless and helpless.

Years later, Russian researchers Volynkina et al,[4] confirmed this conclusion. They recorded tension in the stomach and eye muscles of individuals previously tested and found to be either anxious, normal, or depressed. Records of tension levels in these muscles revealed that anxious people are significantly more tense than normals or depressives, while depressed persons show significantly lower muscle tension levels than normals or the anxiety-prone.

Both Reich and Baker had previously reported finding a breakdown of muscle tonicity and feelings of lethargy in depressed patients. One year before the publication of Baker's book, researchers Rimon et al,[5] reported that depressed persons who improve during one month of psychotherapy show increased muscle tension over those who do not show improvement, and that those individuals experiencing milder depressions have greater muscle tension than those in deep or chronic depression.

In schizophysiology, the failure in communication between reptilian, mammalian, and human brain layers creates conflicted movement — one movement-pattern directed at resolving a need or desire is blocked by an opposing movement-pattern directed at preventing such movement. The result, as Bull's studies of human emotion make so clear, is a set of incompatible muscular responses which are experienced as fear, anger, disgust, and depression.

Body of Evidence

Foreshadowing Bull's insightful studies, as well as the clinical observations of Reich, Baker, and others, Charles Darwin, naturalist, and William James, psychologist and philosopher, espoused a similar theory—more than a century ago. It holds that emotional expressions, such as changes in posture, breathing, or facial displays, are not just the visible signs of an emotion, but compose the emotion itself. The response of a cat when threatened is to raise the fur and arch the back, pulling back the muscles of the face and hissing. This emotional pattern has evolutionary implications in that it functions to make the animal appear larger and more menacing, and thus increases its chances of survival.

This body/mind theory does not maintain that bodily/facial expressions are more important than thoughts or memories in prompting human emotions, but points to the physiology of various bodily expressions as constituents of emotions in their own right. Darwin, for one, considered his work on emotional expression in animals, including humans, as the crowning achievement of the theory of evolution.

Additionally, Darwin noted that energy streams outward toward the body's surface in pleasure, and inward toward the body's core in fear and anxiety, suggesting that these actions played a role in temperature regulation by the circulatory and vascular systems of the body.

He also introduced a polar arrangement whereby emotional states, such as joy and sadness, have associated bodily movements that are also opposite in nature. Many of the same muscles which participate in our wild laughter also participate in our deep sobbing and crying.

Darwin also maintained that conscious attention focused on any part of the body can physically alter it, thereby predating much of contemporary body/mind theory and research which suggests that feelings, emotions, and the healing process itself can be facilitated through active attending.[6]

For William James,[7] *feelings* are the very essence of emotion, and without feelings, the concept of emotion would be empty.

> If we fancy some strong emotion, and then try to abstract from our consciousness all the feelings of its bodily symptoms, we find we have nothing left behind, no 'mind stuff' out of which the emotion can be constituted, and that a cold and neutral state of intellectual perception is all that remains.
>
> — William James, *Psychology*

Our moods, feelings, and emotions, according to James, are more determined by bodily responses than by mental logic, and in this sense, our bodily sensations *are* our emotions, and not just our consciousness of them. "Common sense," James states, "says we are insulted by a rival, are angry and strike ... the more rational statement (however), is that we feel sorry because we cry, angry because we strike, afraid because we tremble ... "

James anticipated many contemporary body/mind theorists in suggesting that emotional reactions can occur which are far removed from the original situation, and that an emotional expression can become destructive to us when it is interrupted in some way. "Stopping the expression of an emotion," he says "often makes it worse. The funniest becomes quite excruciating when we are forbidden by the situation to laugh, and anger pent in by fear turns into ten-fold hate. Expressing either emotion freely, however, gives relief ... "

We all experience life's conflicts and pain but we are not usually aware that our anger, fear, sadness, and so on, are linked to muscular blockages in our lived-body. Often, incompatible movement patterns originate in early childhood traumas and abuses when we stop choosing to act or feel or think in certain ways so as to avoid punishment, frustration, and pain.

Consider little Jennifer, abused and molested at home to the point of preparing to run away. Legs tighten, anger fuels, images form, escape strategies are rehearsed. And yet, there is an alternate terror which freezes the child in conflict: the fear of being alone and hungry and cold. The act of running out of fear is repressed by thoughts of a future filled with even more intense fears and needs. Over time, muscles of the legs become tightly armored, and as such, embody the conflict itself. In this way, our verbal statements of denial are identical with the repressed emotions which become armored into our bodies. These embodied conflicts, as first suggested by Darwin, also disallow the expression of compatible and synchronous movements, such as joy, triumph, and surprise.

Immersed in the confusion, frustration and pain born of our struggle to deny and repress our emotions, we are mostly unaware that the tension created seeks substitute, often destructive, channels of release — in the form of disease, chronic pain, depression, and violence.

A few years following Bull's groundbreaking studies, psychologist Robert Plutchik,[8] in reviewing the relationship between emotions, muscular holding patterns, and human personality concluded that these patterns have personal meaning to us as ways of reducing anxiety, repressing certain emotional tendencies, and denying certain experiences and beliefs. The results of empirical and clinical studies, over the years, have consistently lent support to this thesis.

In one notable study by psychologist M. Sundsvold,[9] he rated four groups of persons diagnosed as neurotic and psychotic on forty-seven purely physical variables and discovered that thirty-four of these measures related to specific psychiatric conditions. Psychotics, for instance, had the greatest deviation from normal posture and muscle elasticity, the greatest resistance to movement, and reported the highest discomfort when touched by another person. Persons labeled neurotic had the most inhibited breathing levels.

In a series of experiments by J. H. Riskind, reported in 1984, subjects were induced to adopt either a slumped, depressed posture, or an upright, confident posture. Then they were assigned a series of insoluble problems to work on. Subjects assigned to the slumped posture persisted less on the tasks than those in the upright posture. Apparently, the slumped posture had produced effects very much like learned helplessness — subjects also reported feeling more stress and frustration in the slumped posture.

In a related study, it was found that subjects induced to assume particular emotional postures and facial expressions were more likely to retrieve memories which corresponded to the specific emotion. In addition to their effects on emotional experience and memory, changes in posture and facial expression induced subjects to change their attitudes and self-descriptions to fit their appearance.[10]

In another study, Osbourne and Swenson[11] correlated tension measures in muscles of the upper face and eyes with individual scores on a personality inventory. They found that those persons with the higher muscle tension levels were, generally, more rigid in their attitudes; more likely to use denial as a psychological defense; more likely to conform to the demands of others; and experienced more anxiety in the presence of others.

Other studies were conducted during therapy sessions. Malmo and Shagass,[12] for instance, recorded muscle tension in the legs and arms of clients during therapy and correlated them with certain themes which arose during the sessions. They discovered that in conversations having to do with sexuality, muscular tension significantly increased in the client's legs. When conversation turned to anger or hostility in the client's life, muscle tension increased in the client's arms. The correlations were direct ones, in that, the more a client denied that sexuality or anger were issues to be dealt with, the more the muscle tension increased in the legs and arms, respectively.

Psychoanalyst Anne Bernstein,[13] based on case studies conducted during psychoanalytic sessions, concluded that chronic back pain, and accompanying muscle spasms, act as a second line of defense against the emergence of repressed emotions — the first line of defense being a general lack of awareness of these feelings and emotions by the client.

Hot Heads

Two of the strongest pieces of evidence in support of the body/mind theory of emotion were published in 1989.

In one, a team of psychologists at Clark University showed that simply having people put their facial muscles in a configuration typical of a given emotion produced that feeling. In the study, volunteers were given the following instruction.

Fear. Raise your eyebrows. And open your eyes wide. Move your whole head back, so that your chin is tucked in a little bit, and let your mouth relax and hang open a little.

Anger. Draw your eyebrows together and down. Contract the muscles at the corner of your jaw by clenching your teeth.

Disgust. Narrow your eyes a bit by squinting a little. Raise your upper lip toward your nostrils, letting your nostrils flair out a little, if that's convenient.

Sadness. Lower your eyebrows, especially the outer corners. With your mouth closed, push up lightly with your lower lip.

By and large, the different facial expressions produced the moods they portray. While simulating the facial expression of anger, for instance, volunteers reported more feelings of anger than of disgust, sadness, or fear. This research was similar to another study conducted in 1983 in which researchers were able to induce happy feelings by having volunteers hold a small pen clenched in their teeth, imitating a smile. When the subjects held the pen in their protruding lips, simulating a pout, they reported feeling unhappy.[14]

In another study conducted by Robert Zajonc at the University of Michigan, volunteers repeated vowel sounds over and over, such as those of a long "eee" which forces a smile, or "ahhh" which imparts a facial expression of surprise. Both induced pleasant feelings in subjects. A long "uuu," on the other hand, put volunteers in their worst mood.

Zajonc theorizes that the connection between facial expression and emotion hinges on the fact that all biochemical processes in the body change their rates as the temperature in the immediate region of the body changes. This includes the activity of neurons and neurotransmitters.

The internal carotid artery, which provides the main supply of blood to the brain, flows through the cavernous sinus of the head. This part of the sinus is laced with veins from the muscles of the face. As facial muscles stretch and tighten, the blood flow to the sinus changes. This, in turn, raises or lowers the temperature of blood flowing into the brain, particularly to the hypothalamus, a structure that regulates both emotion and the body's reaction to heat and cold. Zajonc states, "The hypothalamus is profoundly involved in emotional life. But it also regulates the temperature of the brain and the body. Its dual role is indicated, for instance, by its involvement in shivering, which occurs both in fear and freezing, or in sweating, which is seen during anxiety or excitement, as well as in reaction to excessive heat."[15]

Unhappy expressions, like a frown or a scowl, tighten different sets of facial muscles, which tends to allow more blood into the cavernous sinus. This heats the blood flowing to the brain.

A smile, on the other hand, tightens muscles primarily in the cheeks, and the broader the smile, the tighter these muscles become. This tends to decrease the flow of blood to the sinus, thus cooling the blood that flows to the brain.

Previous research (1983), conducted by Paul Ekman and other psychologists at the University of California Medical School in San Francisco, showed that when people mimic different emotional expressions, or relive a past emotional experience (e.g., anger, fear, sadness, happiness, disgust, and surprise), their bodies produce distinctive physiological patterns, such as changes in temperature, heart rate, and breath rate for each emotion. Heart rate, for instance, increases more in anger than in happiness while fingers are colder in fear than in anger.[16]

Roots of Violence

Other studies lend consistent support to the thesis that tightening the muscles, holding the breath and denying feelings and emotions emanating from the lived-body, not only distorts our perceptions of the world, but tends to make us more reactive to conflict, even as we struggle to repress it.

In a study by Hare,[17] experimental findings strongly suggest that repressing our emotions through muscular holding causes us to become *more* reactive to events which threaten the particular emotions being repressed. Hare, for instance, rated individuals as either *repressors* or *sensitizers*, based on their score on a personality inventory. A repressor was defined as one who tries to deny feelings about a threatening situation, and a sensitizer as one who acknowledges and verbally expresses feelings connected to a threatening event. Researchers recorded muscular tension levels in both groups as subjects sat before a ticking clock knowing they would receive an electric shock every thirty seconds.

Results revealed that the repressors showed the greatest physiological reaction before and during the shocking event, while the sensitizers, who had expressed their fears, both physically and verbally, were significantly less reactive before and during the stress period.

In another study, Grings and Dawson[18] concluded that although repression makes us more reactive to events which threaten us, it does not make us more responsive to coping with these events. In their research, the rate and amplitude of the breath was measured in two groups of subjects who scored either high or low on reality-testing, that is, on their ability to accurately assess and respond to the behavior of others while, at the same time, maintaining the integrity of their own sense-of-self. In a series of stress inducing sessions, it was discovered that individuals high in reality-testing expressed their anxiety more often than individuals low in reality-testing, and responded with greater changes in breathing rate and amplitude which closely paralleled the intensity of the stress inducing stimulation as they received it.

The findings of Nina Bull's research, along with these more recent studies, begin to suggest how the body/mind connection functions in our emotional and mental life, and precisely how repression and denial of lived-body results in: increased stress; emotional over-reaction and potential violence; as well as the inability to accurately perceive and respond to the reality around us and within us. They also point to newer, body-based healing practices which might facilitate synchrophysiology — and the healing of the whole person.

Notes

1. Robert Hall and Thomas Pope. Awareness As Healing, *Lomi Papers*, Summer, 1981, Tomales, CA, pp. 31–37.

2. Paul D. MacLean. Man's Reptilian and Limbic Inheritance, In *A Triune Concept of the Brain and Behaviour*, T. J. Boag and D. Campbell, eds., 1973, University of Toronto Press, Toronto.

3. Bull, Nina. *The Body and Its Mind*, 1962, Las Americas Publishing, New York.

4. Volynkina, G. Y., S. M. Zamakhover and A. N. Timofeiva. An EMG Study of Emotional States, *Psychological Abstracts*, 1971, 17 (4), 49–59.

5. Rimon, R., A. Stenback and E. Huhman. Electromyographic Findings in Depressive Patients, *Journal of Psychosomatic Research*, 1966, 10, 159.

6. Darwin, Charles. *The Expression of the Emotions In Man and Animals*, 1965, University of Chicago Press, Chicago. (Work first published in 1896.)

7. James, William. *Psychology*, 1892, Henry Holt and Company, New York.

8. Plutchik, Robert. The Role of Muscular Tension in Maladjustment, *Journal of General Psychology*, 1954, 50, 45–62.

9. Sundsvold, M. Muscle Tension and Psychopathology, *Psychotherapy and Psychosomatics*, 1975, 26 (4) 219–27.

10. Riskind, J. H. They Stoop to Conquer: Guiding and Self-Regulatory Functions of Physical Posture After Success and Failure, *Journal of Personality and Social Psychology*, 1984, 47, 479–93.

11. Osborne, D. and W. M. Swenson. Muscle Tension and Personality, *Journal of Clinical Psychology*, 1978, 34 (2), 391–92.

12. Malmo, R. B. and C. Shagass. Physiologic Studies of Reaction to Stress in Anxiety and Early Schizophrenia, *Psychosomatic Medicine*, 1949, 11, 9.

13. Bernstein, Anne E. Psychoanalytic Contribution to Etiology of "Back Pain" and "Spinal Disc Syndrome," *Journal of the American Academy of Psychoanalysis*, 1979, 4, 1.

14. Duclos, Sandra E. et al. Emotion-Specific Effects of Facial Expressions and Postures on Emotional Experience, *Journal of Personality and Social Psychology*, 1989, 57 (1) 100–08.

15. Zajonc, R. B., Sheila T. Murphy, and Marita Inglehart. Feeling and Facial Efference: Implications of the Vascular Theory of Emotion, *Psychological Review*, 1989, 96 (3), 395–416.

16. Ekman, Paul, Robert W. Levenson, and Wallace V. Friesen. Autonomic Nervous System Activity Distinguishes Among Emotions, *Science*, September, 1983, 221, 1208–10.

17. Hare, J. Orienting and Defensive Response to Visual Stimuli, *Psychophysiology*, 1973, 10, 453–64.

18. Grings, J. and M. Dawson. *Emotions and Bodily Responses*, 1978, Academic Press, New York.

Suggested Readings

Gazzaniga, M. *The Social Brain: Discovering the Networks of the Mind*, 1985, Basic Books, New York.

Hooper, Judith and Dick Teresi. *The Three Pound Universe*, 1986, Macmillan and Company, New York.

Ornstein, Robert and R. Thompson. *The Amazing Brain*, 1984, Houghton Mifflin, New York.

Pert, C. Emotions in Body, Not Just In Brain. *Brain/Mind Bulletin*, 1986, 11 (4), 1.

Plutchik, Robert. *Emotion: A Psychoevolutionary Synthesis*, 1980, Harper and Row, New York.

Part Three
Bodywork

10

Stress, Mad-ness, and Dis-ease

> The holding back of aggressiveness is in general unhealthy and leads to illness. A person in a fit of rage often demonstrates how the transition from restrained aggressiveness to self-destructiveness is effected, by turning his aggressiveness against himself: he tears his hair or beats his face with his fists — treatment which he would evidently have preferred to apply to someone else. Some portion of self-destructiveness remains permanently within, until it at length succeeds in doing the individual to death, not, perhaps, until his libido has been used up or has become fixated in some disadvantageous way. Thus it may in general be suspected that the *individual* dies of his internal conflicts ... [1]
> — Sigmund Freud, *An Outline of Psychoanalysis*

Not too long ago, the word *psychosomatic* was the only one we had to describe the effect of mind on body in various physical diseases — and the term was often used as a kind of conceptual trash bucket for physical diseases with no apparent physiological basis. To be told by a physician that one's ailment was "psychosomatic" was synonymous to saying, "it's all in your head!" or "you're making it up!"

Today, most standard medical textbooks attribute anywhere from 50 to 80 percent of all diseases to stress-related origins — and large-scale, epidemiological surveys reveal that at least 50 percent of the U.S. population suffers from stress-related disorders.[2]

The breakthrough event which would establish the role of emotion and cognition in disease processes occurred throughout the early 1950s in the laboratory of organic chemist Hans Seleye.

Seleye wondered whether certain traumatic events, such as electric shocks, would cause any physical damage to the rats receiving them. Although, to all appearances, the shocked rats suffered little in the way of harmful effects, Seleye's autopsies revealed significant tissue damage, including broken vessels, shrunken glands and other physical effects. He termed the phenomenon *stress*.[3]

With the publication of Seleye's research findings, the field of psychosomatic medicine appeared to explode in all directions.

Through the 1960s, great emphasis was placed on understanding the variety of bodily changes connected with stress: rise in blood pressure and pulse rate, faster breathing, and increased electrical activity in the brain. Other researchers, reasoning that if stress could turn *on* this reaction, other factors might turn it *off*, studied the effects of biofeedback, muscular relaxation, meditation, and other states of consciousness in controlling stress reactions in the body.

Beginning in the mid-sixties and into the 1970s, researchers went further by focusing on the role played by emotional stressors and personality dynamics in the development of disease states. Psychologist Lawrence LeShan,[4] based on interviews with hundreds of cancer patients, reported that people with certain kinds of personality traits had a higher than average incidence of cancer. Persons with this "cancer personality," LeShan reported, preferred to repress angry, hostile feelings rather than express them; tested low in feelings of self-worth; and harbored deep feelings of helplessness. Interestingly, prior to their diagnosis, many of these cancer-prone subjects had experienced a traumatic personal loss, such as the death of a loved one or a divorce.

In the mid-seventies, researchers Caroline Thomas and K. R. Duszynski,[5] at Johns Hopkins University, added more subtle dimensions to LeShan's thesis that certain personality traits were themselves, *stressors*, which resulted in specific tissue damage and disease. In a longitudinal study of Johns Hopkins Medical School graduates between 1948 and 1964, they reported that one group of students, who had disclosed that they were emotionally distant from one or both parents, were found to have suffered a higher incidence of mental illness, suicide, death from cancer, hypertension and coronary heart disease — decades later.

The question which boggled researcher's minds, at this juncture, was this, "how could emotional repression, low self-esteem, loss of a loved one or emotional distance from parents translate into tissue damage?" After all, my heart doesn't "know" of the death of my loved one; the liver can't "know" of my 'low self-esteem.' Only the human brain had knowledge of these things.

Meanwhile, another phenomenon began to unfold at the Kennedy Space Center where physicians, examining Apollo astronauts during their return from space, found changes in their immunological systems (i.e., the white cell count) that appeared only during the stress connected with reentry to earth. Blood samples taken on the moon, and during travel back to earth showed normal immunological response. Immediately upon reentry and landing, however, the immunological system was depressed — the white cell count was suspiciously low.

By the mid-seventies, the pieces of the puzzle began to fall into place as researchers discovered that the brain is also a gland that secretes hormones which effect the rest of the body, including the immunological system, and that the brain reacts, in turn, to hormones secreted by other glands in the body.

Researchers discovered physiological changes under long-term stress which they termed a stress "cascade": the hypothalamus releases CRH (cortico-tropin releasing hormone) which stimulates the pituitary gland to secrete ACTH (adrenocorticotropic hormone) which, in turn, prompts the adrenal gland to produce cortisol which, in addition to increasing blood sugar and speeding up metabolism, *suppresses the body's immune system.*

Since the discovery of the first opiate-like brain hormone, less than twenty years ago, researchers have discovered at least forty-five separate hormones in the brain, many of which directly effect the immunological system. Studies from a number of laboratories have shown that various stressors can down-regulate the immune response in various animals, including humans. For example, it has been shown that there are nerve endings in different lymphoid organs; that certain hormones such as cortisol can regulate certain aspects of cellular immunity, and that lymphocytes are able to produce certain hormones which, in turn, may have effects on the nervous system.[6]

The long, sought-after body/mind bridge is sighted — and its structure is chemical, its function is informational — and its contribution to a holistic, Body/Mind Psychology is monumental. Today, according to researcher and writer Kenneth Pelletier,[7] we know how " ... a purely physical stressor can influence the higher thought centers, and a mentally or intellectually perceived stressor can generate neurophysiological responses."

Emotional Repression and Immunosuppression

Suppression of the immune system in short-term stress protects us from reacting to, say, the inflammation and swelling of a wound. In so doing, the immunosuppression process works to increase our chances of survival. Soldiers, for instance, often report not being aware of a body wound until well out of danger.

Under conditions of long-term stress, however, this same immunosuppression process can make us more susceptible to disease and dysfunction. Prolonged stress has been shown to suppress physical growth, diminish sex drive, reduce the output of reproductive hormones, and play an important role in cancer, coronary heart disease, asthma, gastrointestinal diseases, migraine headaches, and a host of other disorders.

Central to present day understanding of this body/mind connection are two key hypotheses which, when joined together, suggest a conceptual model of just how physical disease results from mental/emotional stress. The first, termed the *nuclear conflict* hypothesis states that the presence of unconscious conflict involving the expression/repression of primitive emotions, including anger, sadness, fear, and disgust, acts as a central stressor. Like the wound to the soldier in battle, it signals the release of opiate-like chemicals from the brain which suppress the immunological system. Unlike the soldier's wound, however, the stress is ongoing and long-term because the nuclear conflict remains chronically unresolved.

The second, termed the *immunosuppression* hypothesis, states that stress in our life suppresses the immunological system and when a nuclear emotional conflict remains unresolved, this suppression of the immunological system becomes chronic resulting in a breakdown of the body/mind complex in the form of psychosomatic disorders.

Because the impulses are repressed, the corresponding behaviors (e.g., aggression, crying, running, gagging), though physiologically activated, are not brought to expression. We are left suspended, as it were, in a state of muscular preparedness. This state of suspension, between the impulse to act and the impulse to repress action, is the chronic stressor which suppresses our immunological competence.

Each psychosomatic disorder is, to some extent, the outcome of some central emotional conflict. Unconscious inhibition of self-assertive hostile impulses, for instance, appears to play a role in cardiovascular disorders, including heart disease, hypertension, and headaches; while emotional conflicts involving dependency or unfulfilled needs for love and affection are associated with gastrointestinal disorders, including ulcers and colitis.

Other research implicates more subtle stressors. In an ongoing series of research studies by Ronald Glaser et al,[8] at The Ohio State University College of Medicine, the effects of academic stress and loneliness have been documented. In one study, immune competence was measured in a group of medical students one month prior to examinations and during examination days. The results obtained from multiple studies with first and second year medical students showed a significant decrease in the number of and activity level of helper cells and suppressor cells, and in total lymphocyte population during exams.

In a separate study of lymphocyte responsiveness obtained from nonmedicated, psychiatric inpatients divided into high-loneliness and low-loneliness groups, based on scores on the UCLA Loneliness Scale — it was found that subjects in the high-loneliness group had a significantly lower level of immunological competence than the low-loneliness group.

Personality, Samsara, and Dis-ease

From the perspective of a Body/Mind Psychology, we are psychosomatic systems — a certain amount of energy enters the body/mind complex from moment-to-moment—and a like amount of energy seeks release over time. If this entrance/exit equation does not approximate *balance* over time, the result is the high-speed, hyperconscious state of *samsara* — followed, in time, by the development of psychological and psychosomatic disorders—as the weakest link in the system gives way under the burden of chronic, unremitting stress.

Cancer

A number of personality traits and emotional styles have been consistently associated with cancer-prone persons—and a central hypothesis is that people who have trouble acknowledging and expressing strong feelings are more prone to develop cancer than people who typically ventilate their pent-up emotions.

The key defenses appear to involve repression and denial. In one study by Plumb and Holland, for example, only 30 percent of cancer patients *admitted* any discouragement whatever about their future, although many of them had large, inoperable tumors.[9]

More specifically, the way we deal with angry feelings is emerging as particularly important. In a series of research studies which began at Kings College in London, and replicated in studies conducted in U.S. clinics, it was found that women with breast cancer are significantly more likely to repress anger and hostility towards others, while using denial as a psychological defense against the ever-increasing pressures and conflicts experienced. In another study[10] of patients with cancerous and noncancerous lung diseases, researchers described the significant difference leading to cancer as restricted outlet for emotional expression, especially anger.

In an interesting study, Beringheli,[11] connected the development of cancerous tumors to a psychological defense characterized by withdrawal and regression to an earlier developmental period — on both the bodily level (aches and pains to complain about) and the psychological level (helplessness and expectations of aid). Rapid cell growth, as seen in cancer, may be stimulated as a result of this psychosomatic regression to childhood modes of functioning when cell growth is rapid. It is interesting to note that Elsworth Baker, in 1967, theorized that, in addition to orgasm, exercise, and hard work, cell growth played a role in releasing repressed emotions.

A new factor being studied in the search for a cancer-prone personality concerns the repression of feelings of sadness and depression. Typically, cancer prone individuals suffered severe emotional turbulence in childhood in relation to their parents and siblings, with feelings of deep loss, loneliness, and fears of rejection, abandonment, and betrayal. Specifically, they attempt to compensate for these disturbing feelings through approval-seeking behavior directed at those around them. Their insatiable need for acceptance and affection creates an ongoing frustration that eventually leads to self-criticality, self-hatred, a sense of helplessness, and finally, to bouts of chronic anxiety, depression, and hopelessness.[12] In a recent longitudinal study of 2,000 middle-aged men who were administered a multimodal personality inventory (i.e., MMPI), the depression score was associated with increased risk of death by cancer seventeen years later.[13]

Heart Disease

In a series of research studies begun in 1974, Friedman and Rosenman[14] have convincingly uncovered a personality pattern among individuals prone to coronary heart disease and heart ailments. Termed the *Type A* personality pattern, it is characterized by an excessively competitive drive, impatience, aggressiveness, and a chronic sense of time-urgency.

This individual speaks explosively and hurriedly, walks, eats, and moves rapidly, and often sets unnecessary deadlines while doing more than one thing at a time. The Type A person attributes personal success to speed and often reports feeling guilty or bored when relaxing. They tend to evaluate others, as well as themselves, in terms of numbers, such as amount of money earned, and are often preoccupied with acquiring "things." They often reveal certain nervous gestures, such as facial twitches, fist-clenching, and table banging.

In one study of 1,674 volunteers from Framington, Massachusetts, who were followed for nearly a decade,[15] it was discovered that
women who developed coronary heart disease scored significantly
higher in Type A assessments and were less likely to acknowledge and
express their angry feelings. Working women were almost twice as
likely to suffer from heart disease if they exhibited Type A characteristics. Among homemakers, heart disease was almost three times more
likely for women with Type A behavioral characteristics.

High Blood Pressure

Hypertension or high blood pressure is a major contributor to
heart disease and is the most common major chronic disease in the
United States today.

Clinical research consistently reveals hypertensives as persons
emotionally on edge most of the time with wide variability in blood
pressure readings. The central hypothesis concerns the repression of
chronic anger and the findings of recent research support this hypothesis.

According to this theory, hypertensives experience chronic, repressed anger based on their inability to assert themselves in a so-
cially constructive manner. People low in assertiveness skill tend to be
mistreated by others, fail to express their anger, and are less compe-
tent in having their needs met. There is growing evidence that combinations of assertiveness, relaxation, meditation, and biofeedback
training can have particularly positive, long-term effects on lowering
blood pressure.[16]

Headaches

Headaches are the most commonly reported bodily complaint—
about 80 percent of Americans suffer from at least one headache per
year and nearly 20 percent visit a physician with headache as their pre-
senting complaint. Headaches differ in duration and intensity — from
tension headaches and cluster headaches to often highly debilitating
migraine headaches. Although causes may differ, states of prolonged
chronic anxiety seem to be common among headache sufferers—and
seem to occur in response to stressful situations.[17]

The migraine-prone individual is often a rigid, perfectionistic,
highly intelligent person whose achievement needs are set so high as
to be unattainable. The ongoing frustration creates angry, hostile feelings which are often directed toward others in the form of blame.

Frontal headaches, according to Baker, often result from ocular armoring where the forehead is muscularly frozen in a raised position expressing anxiety or suspicion. Headaches in the back of the head—occipital headaches—are associated with armoring of the muscles of the upper neck produced by a chronic "ducking" attitude based on fear of being attacked from behind.

Reports suggest that the use of various bodywork techniques (e.g., acupressure, acupuncture, shiatsu), along with assertiveness training, biofeedback, and cognitive restructuring methods, are effective in the treatment of headaches.[18]

Asthma

People with asthma chronically wheeze, cough, and have great difficulty in breathing. They report feelings of constriction in the chest and apprehension. According to one major hypothesis, asthmatics share a common personality type and similar unconscious conflicts.

The psychological component in asthma involves an individual who feels helpless, but who represses the *cry* for help out of fear of rejection and abandonment. The asthmatic is, often, overly dependent, whining, demanding, and sometimes, angry and hostile toward loved ones—but denying these hostile feelings.

In one study conducted with asthmatic children in Denver, Colorado,[19] it was found that parents of asthmatic children are over-controlling people who create an emotionally tense and conflicted home environment for their offspring. In a more recent study,[20] it was found that children who died of asthma were depressed and in emotional conflict with their parents, as well as the medical personnel treating them.

The asthmatic reaction is due to parasympathetic over-stimulation — a response to underlying chronic anxiety. This results in contraction of the bronchioles and interference with breathing. Baker states, "There is always a great deal of rage repressed in asthmatics, and when it is expressed, the attack is relieved."

Gastrointestinal Disorders

These disorders involve stress-related abnormalities of the digestive system, including diarrhea, constipation, ulcers, and colitis.

Peptic ulcers are often found in persons who tend to over-emphasize their independence while harboring strong dependency needs. They reveal strong blockage in the diaphragm which in turn contracts the mucous membranes of the stomach — interfering with the flow of blood to the abdominal area. Persons with ulcers sometimes reveal a deep sense of responsibility, a strong drive, and repressed feelings of anxiety and hostility. Studies of adolescents reveal that a recent separation or loss is often associated with the onset of peptic ulcers.[21]

The psychological component in *colitis* involves an individual who is perfectionistic, obsessive, hypersensitive, and who tends to turn anger inward, on the self, which often results in chronic depression. The colitis sufferer feels driven to please others, while, at the same time, feeling resentment at their demands. They often present an outward calm and bravery in spite of deep underlying anxiety. The mechanism that produces colitis is believed to be similar to that appearing in asthma — an overstimulation of the parasympathetic nervous system.

Herpes

Herpes, from the Greek, *herpein*, "to creep," applies to several types of skin eruptions characterized by formation of blisters which develop in a spreading or creeping fashion. Very recent research links stress and the appearance, duration, and intensity of the herpes virus infection to alterations in cellular immunity.

Normally, after a herpes virus outbreak, the virus is repressed in a latent state in certain host cells. Any form of immunosuppression, whether brought on by the presence of another active virus in the system, or after radiation treatments in cancer patients, or through social or personal stressors, increases the probability of another virus outbreak.

In one study, reported by Glaser and Kiecolt-Glaser,[22] it was found that there was an increased risk for infection by the Epstein-Barr virus in West Point cadets connected to certain psychological risk factors, including poorer academic performance, overachieving levels of motivation, and, having a father who was an overachiever. In a related study, it was found that unhappiness among nursing students was a predictor for outbreak of herpes virus on the lips of the vagina, as was academic stress and loneliness in other subject populations.

Acquired Immune Deficiency Syndrome (AIDS)

The high-risk populations for acquired immune deficiency syndrome (AIDS) and AIDS-related complex (ARC) include homosexual men and intravenous drug abusers — both of whom may be more psychologically stressed groups because of societal and sociological pressures. Furthermore, these populations, which are aware of the AIDS association with homosexuality and intravenous drug use are under additional psychological stress because of the knowledge of the association of this devastating illness with their practices.

As Glaser and Kiecolt-Glaser state in summarizing their extensive research on the effects of various stressors on immunological competence, "Suffice it to say that if the distress associated with taking examinations (academic stress) is sufficient to affect cell-mediated immunity, then the stress associated with the social interactions of the gay community could have immunological consequences." (p. 209)

As in the case of herpes, simply having the virus and carrying it in T lymphocytes does not necessarily imply that a person will have clinical disease — only a certain percentage of persons with AIDS-related complex become AIDS patients.

What determines the clinical course of the disease is not known, precisely, but it appears possible that any suppression of the immune response could result in an impact on the virus and the lymphocyte such that the virus could be reactivated from the latently infected lymphocytes. This reactivated virus could then infect other lymphocytes. If this occurs in an individual whose immune system is less efficient than normal, brought on, perhaps, by the chronic stress associated with the fear of social ostracism and retribution, the appearance, duration, and severity of clinical symptoms could be directly affected.

In a recent presentation[23] at California State University, Sacramento, a panel of healthy participants with AIDS, ARC, and HIV +, report that a combination of healing methods, including Sufi meditation, breathing exercises, physical awareness and movement, nutrition and immuno-enhancing visualization has significantly improved, not only their immunological competence in controlling the AIDS virus, but the overall quality of their lives.

Whether psychological stress can precipitate the development of AIDS in individuals with the AIDS-related complex, and, as with the herpes virus, affect the rate of appearance, duration, and severity of clinical symptoms, remains speculative at this time. Further research will be necessary to determine whether this is the case.

Today, with ever-growing understanding of how body processes interact with mental processes, researchers are investigating numerous disease states for possible stress-related origins. In concert with this explosion of interest in psychosomatic theory and research, a new vocabulary is emerging, which includes concepts such as *psychoneu-roimmunology, behavioral medicine, immunosuppression, behavioral anesthesiology, immunomodulation* and *psychoneuroimmunoenhancement* — all reflections of an interstratified, more holistic approach to the healing arts.

There can be little doubt that emotional repression, personality make-up, and stress-inducing attitudes and beliefs can function as chronic internal stressors which, in turn, significantly decrease the competence of the immunological system, and thus, play a significant role in the development of certain physical diseases and forms of emotional dysfunction.

Body/Mind Psychology must continue to focus research of this very important body/mind connection, and work to develop new healing regimens which fully utilize these deepening discoveries and insights.

Notes

1. Freud, Sigmund. *An Outline of Psychoanalysis*, 1949, W. W. Norton and Company, New York, p. 22.

2. Bakal, Donald A. *Psychology and Medicine: Psychobiological Dimensions of Health and Illness*, 1979, Springer Publications, New York.

3. Seleye, Hans. *The Stress of Life*, 1956, McGraw-Hill Publishing Co., New York.

4. LeShan, Lawrence L. and R. E. Worthington. Personality as a Factor in Pathogenesis of Cancer: Review of Literature, *British Journal of Medical Psychology*, 1956, 29, 29.

5. Thomas, Carolyn B. and K. R. Duszynshi. Closeness to Parents and the Family Constellation in a Prospective Study of Five Disease States: Suicide, Mental Illness, Malignant Tumor, Hypertension, and Coronary Heart Disease, *Johns Hopkins Medical Journal*, 1974, 134, 251 – 69.

6. Ader, R. R. *Psychoneuroimmunology*, 1985, Academic Press, New York.

7. Pelletier, Kenneth. *Mind As Healer, Mind As Slayer*, 1971, Dell Publishers, New York.

8. Glaser, Ronald and Janice Kiecolt-Glaser. Stress-Associated Immune Suppression and Acquired Immune Deficiency Syndrome (AIDS), In *Psychological, Neuropsychiatric and Substance Abuse Aspects of AIDS*, T. Peter Bridge et al, eds., 1988, Raven Press, New York, 203 – 15.

9. Plumb, M. M. and J. Holland. Comparative Studies of Psychological Function in Patients with Advanced Cancer. I. Self-reported depressive symptoms. *Psychosomatic Medicine*, 1977, 39, 264, 276.

10. Greer, S. and T. Morris. Psychological Attributes of Women with Breast Cancer: A Controlled Study. *Journal of Psychosomatic Research*, 1975, 19, 147–53.

11. Beringheli, F. Towards An Understanding of Cancer, *International Mental Health Research Newsletter,* 1974, 16, 36.

12. See n. 7 above.

13. Persky, V. W., J. Kempthorne-Rawson and R. B. Shekelle. Personality and Risk of Cancer: Twenty-year Follow-up of the Western Electric Study, 1984, *Psychosomatic Medicine*, 49, 435–449.

14. Friedman, M. and R. H. Rosenman. *Type A Behavior and Your Heart*, 1976, Fawcett Publications, New York.

15. Haynes, S. G., M. Feinleib and W. B. Kannel. The Relationship of Psychological Factors to Coronary Heart Disease in the Framington Study: Eight Year Incidence of Coronary Heart Disease, *American Journal of Epedimiology*, 1980, 111, 37–58.

16. Chesney, M. A. and R. H. Rosenman, eds. *Anger and Hostility in Cardiovascular and Behavioral Disorders*, 1985, Hemisphere Publishing, Washington, D.C.

17. Jacob, R. G., R. Wing, and A. P. Shapiro. The Behavioral Treatment of Hypertension: Long-term Effects. *Behavior Therapy*, 1987, 18, 325–352.

18. Thompson, T. L. II. Headache, In *Comprehensive Textbook of Psychiatry*, H. I. Kaplan and B. J. Sadock, eds., 1982, Williams and Wilkins, Baltimore, Maryland.

19. Purcell, K. et al. The Effect on Asthma in Children of Experimental Separation from the Family, *Psychosomatic Medicine*, 1969, 31, 144–64.

20. Strunk, R. C. et al. Physiologic and Psychological Characteristics Associated with Deaths Due to Asthma in Childhood: A Case-controlled Study. *Journal of the American Medical Association*, 1985, 254, 1193–98.

21. Ackerman, S. H., S. Manaker and M. I. Cohen. Recent Separation and the Onset of Peptic Ulcer Disease in Older Children and Adolescents. *Psychosomatic Medicine*, 1981, 43, 305–10.

22. See n. 8 above.

23. O'Riordan, Linda and Maktab Tarighe Oveyssi Shahmaghsoudi. *The Art of Sufi Healing as Applied to AIDS*, Presentation at California State University, Sacramento, California, August 5, 1989, Sacramento AIDS Foundation.

Suggested Readings

Achterberg, J. *Imagery and Healing*, 1985, Shambhala, Boston.

Ader, R. Behaviorally Conditioned Modulation of Immunity. In R. Guillemin, M. Cohn and T. Melnechuk, eds. *Neural Modulation of Immunity*, 1985, Raven Press.

Alexander, F. *Psychosomatic Medicine*, 1950, Norton, New York.

Barber, T. X. Hypnosis, Suggestions and Psychosomatic Phenomena: A New Look from the Standpoint of Recent Experimental Studies, *American Journal of Clinical Hypnosis*, 1978, 21 (1), 13–27.

Cousins, N. *Anatomy of an Illness as Perceived by the Patient*, 1979, Norton, New York.

Goldberger, L. and S. Breznitz, eds. *Handbook of Stress*, 1982, MacMillan, New York.

Jenkins, C., R. H. Rosenman, and S. J. Zyzanski. Predictions of Coronary Heart Disease by a Test for Coronary-Prone Behavior, 1974, *New England Journal of Medicine*, 23, 1271–75.

LeShan, Lawrence. *You Can Fight for Your Life*, 1977, Evans and Co., New York.

Locke, S. et al. Life Change Stress, Psychiatric Symptoms, and Natural Killer-cell Activity, *Psychosomatic Medicine*, 1984, 46, 441–53.

Maclean, D. and S. Reichlin. Neuroendocrinology and the Immune Process. In R. Ader, ed. *Psychoneuroimmunology*, Academic Press, New York.

Margolis, C. Hypnotic Imagery with Cancer Patients. *The American Journal of Clinical Hypnosis*, 1982, 25 (3), 475–519.

Meares, A. A Form of Intensive Meditation Associated with the Regression of Cancer. *The American Journal of Clinical Hypnosis*, 1983, 25, (3), 114–21.

Melnechuk, T. Neuroimmunology: Crossroads Between Behavior and Disease. Reports on Selected Conferences and Workshops. *Advances*, 1985, 2 (3), Summer.

Rossi, Ernest Lawrence. *The Psychobiology of Mind-Body Healing*, 1986, W. W. Norton, New York.

Shavit, Y. et al. Stress, Opioid, the Immune System, and Cancer. *The Journal of Immunology*, 1985, 135 (2), 334–37.

Silberner, J. A New Look at Arthritis Origins, *Science News*, 1985, 127 (23), 358–59.

Simonton, O., S. Simonton and J. Creighton. *Getting Well Again*, 1978, J. B. Tarcher, New York.

Solomon, G. The Emerging Field of Psychoneuroimmunology with a Special Note on AIDS, 1985, *Advances*, 2, Winter, 6–19.

11

Anatomy Lessons

The messages that make up our emotional and mental life must be routed through the tissues of the body. Each segment of our anatomy, each zone of muscles and tissue, each organ, has a unique function in the overall system. Clinical researchers and therapists, working from the perspective of a Body/Mind Psychology, have begun tracking the common associations between body characteristics and the characteristics of our mental and emotional life.

In a survey by King,[1] a large number of these researchers and therapists were questioned regarding specific body/personality relationships and significant agreement was found among respondents. Some of the relationships receiving the highest agreement ratings are presented below:

Body Characteristic	Personality Trait	Rating
Feet solidly on ground	Security	93%
Raised shoulders	Fear	91%
Downward turned mouth	Depression	91%
Perpetual smile	Negative Attitudes	88%
Tight jaw	Anger	87%
Forward pulled shoulders	Protection	84%
Tight chin	Sadness	80%
Tense shoulder blades	Anger	76%
Tense back	Anger	75%
Head held at angle	Avoidance	72%
Tight legs	Rigidity	68%
Tight arms	Anger	66%

The following section surveys what various researchers, theorists and therapists have speculated as to the relationship between certain areas of the body and particular personality traits, attitudes, and forms of repression.

Eyes

The eyes are often thought of as windows into the emotional state
of a person: the absence of eye contact signals high anxiety; gaze decreases with disliking and increases with liking of another; avoiding
the gaze of another may signal appeasement to aggression; and constant gaze from within two feet of another induces anxiety.[2]

Armoring of the eye muscles consists of contractions and im-
mobilization of the eye itself, eye lids, forehead, and tear glands. This
armoring of the eyes is most often seen in persons who, from an early
age, have been unable to cry, and who view the world with anxiety and
suspicion. Alexander Lowen[3] notes that wide open eyes, when combined with a high, tight brow, express apprehension, panic, and fear.
Reich,[4] along with Kurtz and Prestera,[5] also associate high eye brows
with anxiety and fear and report that stress in living is, often, expressed as knots between the eyes.

Elsworth Baker[6] places great emphasis on the eyes as the first
area of the body to become armored or traumatized. He states, "Developmental restrictions in this zone are a severe handicap because
without its full growth no adequate perspective on the environment or
even of self is ever attained."

Chronic ocular holding gives the appearance of "hard eyes"
which creates distorted perspective and, in the extreme, may destroy
binocular disparity and, thereby, depth perception. This causes the individual to give exaggerated importance to surface appearances, without a surrounding context. Such persons may see hate, anger, or fear
in other people and feel these expressions are directed at them alone.
They may become deeply frightened because they lack contextual understanding that these emotions are not carried out by most persons.
Thus, ocular holding is seen by Baker as common to states of paranoia
and other schizophrenic conditions where the individual is unable to
open the eyes wide and appears, instead, to be peering through the
holes of a false face.

Baker's speculations are supported in a study by I. K.
Moustgaard[7] which found that increased muscular tension in the ex-
trinsic muscles of the eye can effect "egocentric localization." This refers to the fact that the factual visual median point is displaced in the
direction of the side of the body where muscular tension is highest. Increased ocular tension restrains visual feedback to the brain creating
an ongoing perceptual distortion for the individual.

Jaws

Taken together, researchers and therapists associate chronic tension in the muscles of the jaw with unfinished business connected to anger, sadness, and the holding back of vocal and verbal expression of these emotions.

According to psychologist Will Schutz,[8] chronic muscle tensions are related to feelings that are suspended between the preparation and performance stages — and in the case of the muscles of the jaw, when tense, are inhibiting anger and the impulse to bite. Baker relates jaw tension to repressed anger and sadness and finds this holding pattern common to depressive states. Lowen also relates jaw tension to anger and the biting reflex. Dychtwald[9] views jaw tension primarily as holding back the impulse to speak out and assert oneself.

Arms

Most theorists view chronic tension in the arms as connected to an inability to reach out to others and to the surrounding environment to get what we need, as well as to an inability to push away or break through obstacles which block satisfaction of our needs and wants or threaten to hurt us.

Schutz attributes tense upper arms to an inability to embrace others and sustain intimate contact. Lowen adds to this the inability to give of oneself. Kurtz and Prestera view chronically tense arms as inhibiting the expression of anger and rage, while flaccid, underdeveloped arms reflect an inability to reach out to others. Lowen suggests that underdeveloped arms result from shoulder tensions that block the flow of blood and tender feelings from reaching the arms.

Deutsch's[10] classic studies of the postures and gestures of clients in psychotherapy sessions, resulted in the following associations between arms gestures and psychological attitude. (See page 102.)

Shoulders

Retracted shoulders, according to most clinical researchers, are associated with repressed anger. Dychtwald, for one, reports that retracted shoulders express a chronic conflict in the person between striking out and holding back angry feelings. Similarly, Reich views re-

Posture	Psychological Attitude
Hands uplifted	Craving for dependency and support
Arms lifted in boxing position	Anger, aggressive impulses
Hand covering or held over head	Craving for protection, guilt over hostility
Hands kept under neck	Guilt over masturbation
Arms flexed, held in pocket	Self-confidence
Arms stretched backward	Longing for affection
Arms held folded over chest	Protective, fear of letting go of anger
Hands clasped over abdomen	Fear of loss
Hands held over genitals	Conflicted sexual desires

tracted shoulders as holding back in a concerted effort to maintain self-control in the face of pent-up feelings of anger and rage.

Rounded or bowed shoulders are associated with a sense of being overburdened, as if one were carrying the weight of the world on one's back. According to Lowen, and Kurtz and Prestera, rounded shoulders often reveal a person who took on difficult responsibilities too early in life — before being physically or emotionally prepared to do so. Schutz and Dychtwald agree that rounded shoulders suggest a correlation between having responsibilities beyond one's capacity to "handle" them.

Shoulders that are pulled upward are associated with fear, anxiety, apprehension, and a tendency toward protection of self. Most theorists view upward pulled shoulders as part of a reflexive startle response which includes holding the breath, dilation of the pupils, evacuation of bowels and bladder, muscular immobility and turtling of the head into uplifted shoulder blades in an effort at protection.

We tend to raise our shoulders toward our ears when frightened. When the startle reflex is discharged, however, the shoulders relax once again. But if there is an inability to escape the fear-inducing situation, our shoulders remain raised in a chronic attitude of fright and fearfulness.

Virtually every clinical researcher surveyed lends support to Bull's experimental finding that when our musculature is rigidly held in a particular emotional expression, we find it all but impossible to experience any other emotional state. Baker, Lowen, and Kurtz and Prestera, for example, maintain that the individual suspended in the startle posture, with raised shoulders, will tend to project this somaticized fear into situations which are, often, totally unrelated to the original fear-inducing situation. In mild cases, partial muscular holding contributes to attacks of free-floating anxiety while extreme cases of chronic holding contributes to devastating paranoid feelings and ideas.

Chest and Diaphragm

Virtually every major theorist and researcher reviewed, including Reich, Baker, and Lowen, are in agreement that chronic holding of the diaphragm and intercostal muscles of the chest is associated with an attempt to repress various emotions by lessening the amount of energy available to the rest of the body. Fear of internal stressors, namely, our own emotions and thoughts, contributes to "holding the breath" — as seen in the startle reflex. By cutting the oxygen supply, we seek to "cool down" the entire body/mind complex.

Lowen essentially defines *armoring* as the muscular binding of anxiety which involves contraction of the diaphragm and chest muscles. He states, " ... the front of the body is hard. It is the hypertonicity of the chest wall in particular that is essential to an armor ... by reducing respirations through an unconscious control over the muscles of the front of the body."

Psychotherapist Alyssa Hall[11] states that " ... chest breathing often occurs when we are changing emotional states; becoming agitated with anger, choking with sadness, gasping with surprise, or holding our breath in fear. Our breath becomes higher and more shallow when we feel anxious, self-conscious or inferior." Deep breathing, that is, breathing which includes movement of the abdomen and diaphragm, according to Hall, is more related to states of calm, rest, meditation, and sleep. This form of breathing, she suggests, allows us to be more receptive, grounded, and assured.

In his book, *Gestalt Therapy*, Fritz Perls[12] states,

The neurotic ... simply cannot breathe — for unaware of what he is doing ... maintains against his breathing a system of motor tensions, such as tightening the diaphragm against tendencies to sob or express disgust, tightening the throat against tendencies to shriek, sticking out the chest to appear substantial, holding back the aggression of the shoulders ... He is utterly incapable of a complete, unforced exhalation. Instead, his breath comes out in uneven spurts — staircase breathing — and it may stop, as if bumping into a wall, long before thorough emptying of the lungs ...

In discussing bodywork techniques helpful in relieving acute and chronic anxiety, Perls states " ... a partial relief of any given instance of anxiety can be obtained, paradoxically, by tightening even further the narrowness of the chest instead of resisting it. By this narrowing of the chest the person forces himself to change from a thoracic to a more abdominal (deeper) breathing. Of course, this measure does not result in any permanent changes in anxiety proneness. In order for that to occur a modification of the underlying muscular hypertonicity has to take place, and such a modification would imply release of the excitement and affects being arrested by these very hypertonicity patterns."

Generally, therapists and theorists are in agreement that body-work directed at loosening and softening the muscles of the chest has two major effects: one involves release of the most recently repressed emotion — which often occurs as movement and elasticity of the mus-culature increases, and concurrently, an increase in oxygen intake, in-creased physical activity, and a general renewal of vitality and moti-vation in the individual. For these reasons, initial sessions of body/ mind psychotherapy are often directed toward mobilizing the breath-ing mechanism and increasing the client's awareness of the breathing pattern.

Pelvis

Most theorists, beginning with Wilhelm Reich, report that chronic muscular holding in the pelvis, buttocks, and legs is associ-ated with sexual anxiety and repression of sexual sensations emanat-ing from this zone of the body — or the result of a protective muscular response to physical abuse involving the buttocks.

Reich maintained that tension in the adductor muscles of the thigh, as well as pelvic muscles, such as the psoas, often express sex-ual conflict or emotional asexuality—which may cause back pain, erec-tive impotence, premature ejaculation, as well as uterine and rectal disorders. Likewise, Alexander Lowen maintains that the retracted pel-vis is an attempt at the repression of genital sensations and he attri-butes this response to the divorce of love from sexual feelings. This split is achieved by stopping tender feelings of the heart from mixing with sexual streamings from the pelvis.

Legs and Feet

The structure and positioning of the legs and feet express our sense of being meaningfully grounded in reality — our personal *under-standing*. Kurtz and Prestera state, "There is an intimate connection between feeling the ground with our feet and being in touch with reality." Stanley Keleman, Richard Strozzi-Heckler,[13] and Alexander Lowen, who coined the term, *grounding*, view tight, stiff legs, muscular holding in the feet and toes, and locked knees, as our attempt to create feelings of security whenever we perceive ourselves to be standing on unsure ground.

Lowen, Keleman, Heckler, and others, have developed elaborate exercises and stress postures directed at grounding the person in reality — by increasing contact between the feet and earth, moment to moment. Heckler's dynamic approach, termed *centering*, involves practice of the ancient martial art of Aikido, to facilitate the body/mind experience. Similar to grounding, centering involves intimate, ongoing contact with the ground. Heckler states, " . . . center is a state of being that is not confined to a certain posture or a constantly held image. Ultimately, center is an inner subjective state that is manifested through the body — a reference point to return to, so we can relate to our life situation in a complete way."

Upper Body/Lower Body

Most major theorists, including Reich, Baker, Lowen and Hall, view the top half of the body as the functionally "public" body, having to do with sensing, speaking, thinking, social feelings, and emotions. The area below the waist is viewed as functionally "private" body, having to do with sexuality, elimination, passion, and our capacity for remaining grounded in reality. In short, the upper half of the body deals primarily with the external world while the lower half expresses our relationship to our inner, private world.

In comparing the upper and lower halves of the body, and the congruity or incongruity between them, a therapist may speculate on the relationship between the outer and inner worlds of the individual. As an example, a person who reveals a well-developed upper body and a somewhat age-regressed, underdeveloped lower body, might offer this differential as a clue to an inner conflict between the person's overdeveloped social image, and the individual's underdeveloped personal understanding.

Left Body/Right Body

Theorists and therapists polled in the study by King showed a high degree of agreement that the right side of the body is "masculine" (75 percent), while the left side of the body is "feminine" (75 percent).

This agreement results from decades of brain research which reveals that the left hemisphere of the human brain — which controls the right side of the body — has to do with linear, analytic thinking functions. While the right hemisphere of the brain — which controls the left side of the body — has to do with feelings, emotions and unconscious processes. Referring to these functions as masculine and feminine derives from the theory of Depth Psychology advanced by Carl Jung.

Psychotherapist Thomas Hanna,[14] for one, suggests that the difference in shape and positioning of the two sides of the body expresses the relationship between our thinking versus feeling functions. For instance, when the left shoulder and hip are held higher as the result of a generally greater tension level than is observed on the right side of the body, this may suggest that the individual is anxious in dealing with feelings and emotions, and more predisposed to thinking and strategizing in dealing with life's problems and conflicts. The same might be said of body *torque* — an overall tension pattern on one side of the body which pulls that side of the body forward.

In concluding this rather cursory survey, it should be noted that just as a therapist or counselor might use the results of a personality test to offer clues as to the history of the client, personality make-up, and to the direction that therapy might take; observations of the body itself, its posture, gestures, and muscular holding patterns, provide an additional array of clues and insights into the processes of healing, communication, and personal growth.

It should also be noted that the theorists cited in this body of evidence base their conclusions on clinical observations of clients seen in therapy. Empirical studies, as reviewed in previous chapters, lend support to their speculations, but in a general way. Direct and concrete empirical studies of this aspect of the body/mind connection remain scant in number.

On the other hand, the degree of agreement among clinical observers is nothing short of impressive. There is beauty in the simplicity of connecting the biological function of body parts to the psychological functioning of the whole person. We don't chew, or bite, or kiss, or speak with our toes. Nor do we jump, and skip, and run, and dance with our jaws. If I chronically tense my jaw muscles, lessen their movement, and perhaps, create pain by doing so, this reveals something about me, my history, my conflicts, and my own body-of-knowledge.

Notes

1. King, C. A. An Investigation of Selected Associations Between Personality Traits and Human Muscular Skeletal Structure, *Doctoral Dissertation*, 1972, University of Miami, Coral Gables, Florida.

2. Bowers, John Waite, Sandra M. Metts and W. Thomas Duncanson. Emotion and Interpersonal Communication, In *Handbook of Interpersonal Communciation*, Mark L. Knapp and Gerald Miller, eds., 1985, Sage Publications, Beverly Hills, California, p. 524.

3. Lowen Alexander. *The Betrayal of the Body*, 1969, Macmillan and Company, New York.

4. Reich, Wilhelm. *Character Analysis*, 1933, Orgone Institute Press, Ansonia Station, New York.

5. Kurtz, Ron and Hector Prestera. *The Body Reveals*, 1984, Harper and Row, New York.

6. Baker, Elsworth. *Man in the Trap*, 1967, Macmillan and Company, New York.

7. Moustgaard, I. K. Perception and Tonus, *Scandinavian Journal of Psychology*, 1975, 16 (1), 55–64.

8. Shutz, Will. *Here Comes Everybody*, 1972, Harper and Row, New York.

9. Dychtwald, Ken. *Bodymind*, 1978, Jove Publications, New York.

10. Deutsch, F. Analysis of Postural Behavior, *Psychoanalytic Quarterly*, 1947, 16, 195–213. Also, Analytic Posturology, *Psychoanalytic Quarterly*, 1952, 21, 196–214.

11. Hall, Alyssa. Breathing Awareness, *Lomi Papers*, 1979, Tomales, CA.

12. Perls, Frederick, Ralph Hefferline and Paul Goodman. *Gestalt Therapy*, 1951, Julian Press, New York.

13. Strozzi-Heckler, Richard. *Anatomy of Change*, 1984, Shambhala Publications, Boston.

14. Hanna, Thomas. *The Body of Life*, 1980, Alfred A. Knopf, New York.

Suggested Readings

Alexander, F. M. *The Resurrection of the Body*, 1974, Dell Publishing/Delta, New York.

Lowen, Alexander. *Bioenergetics*, 1975, Penquin Books, New York.

Lowen, Alexander. *Fear of Life*, 1980, Macmillan and Company, New York.

Pesso, A. *Experience In Action: A Psychomotor Psychology*, 1973, NYU Press, New York.

12

Body Reading

The body's life is the life of sensations and emotions. The body feels real hunger, real thirst, real joy in the sun or snow, real pleasure in the smell of roses or the look of a lilac bush; real anger, real sorrow, real tenderness, real warmth, real passion, real hate, real grief. All the emotions belong to the body and are only recognized by the mind.

—D. H. Lawrence

Obviously, the number of observations a therapist might make in reading another's body is potentially limitless. The readings presented here, from each of three points of view, are meant to communicate more of a flavor as to how a body reading might proceed rather than attempt to exhaust the many possibilities.

Jennifer

Jennifer is a twenty-nine year old, married woman with two young children. Referred by her family physician, she complained of chronic feelings of depression, suicidal fantasies, non-orgasmic sexual response, general lethargy, panic attacks, and spontaneous bouts of crying and sobbing.

She reported one suicide attempt at the age of thirteen following her first petting session with a boyfriend, also thirteen years of age. Her mother was also in the process of divorcing her alcoholic husband, Jennifer's stepfather, during the same period. Jennifer's biological father was killed in an airline accident within months of her birth. "Looking back," she said, "I've never really known what it's like to be happy ... but at least after that suicide attempt, I thought I could keep it under control. Now, I don't know anymore. (Pause.) During the past year, I just don't seem to care about myself — doesn't seem worth it. (Touching her blouse and hair.) Well, just look for yourself — my hair is ugly — and, well ... (Tears welling.) ... I'm tired of just getting through my life."

She said she was close to her husband, Gary, whom she described as the dominant, decision-maker in the family — but she was concerned that her " ... down-moods and negativity" would sooner or later take their toll on her family life. She reported that she was sexually passive and non-orgasmic with Gary — and had never experienced orgasm. When queried about sexual self-stimulation, Jennifer said, "I know it's not cool to say, but the few times I've tried it, it kind of disgusted me." Jennifer described her two children, Chantal, age seven, and Brian, age three, as healthy and secure.

Jennifer reported frequent headaches, neck aches, and lower back pain and difficulty sleeping with terrifying nightmares which she could only vaguely recall. "I don't remember much about the dreams," she said, " ... only that I'm either a little girl in them, or I'm grown-up watching a young girl — and I always wake up from them sweaty and very frightened."

She reported no substance abuse in either herself or her husband — but complained of loss of appetite apparently connected to gastrointestinal upsets which included diarrhea, stomach pains, and waves of nausea. Jennifer experienced irregular menstrual cycles.

A high school graduate with more than two years of college courses to her credit, Jennifer reported once holding hopes of becoming a nurse. Working as a full-time homemaker during the past ten years, Jennifer said, "With the children getting older, I think about getting a job sometimes — but then I wonder what I could even do ... and I don't have a clue as to how I'd go about it ... or even if I want to ... (Pause) ... there I go again, never really making a decision about anything."

Reading of Jennifer's body patterning will be made from three different perspectives: the *physical*, or the way Jennifer's body is aligned in relationship to the gravitational field; the *psychological*, or the way Jennifer's body structure and positioning reveals chronic tension-patterns, and the role they may play in her emotional and cognitive life; and the *therapeutic*, or the way in which Jennifer's experience of herself and others suggests specific personal conflicts and how these observations might best lend themselves to the healing process.

The Physical Profile

The simulated profile of Jennifer's body[1] reveals her relationship to the physical ground which she inhabits: the way her bodily misalignments create muscular tension-patterns which might constrict her expressive movement and, in the extreme, be the source of chronic pain and discomfort.

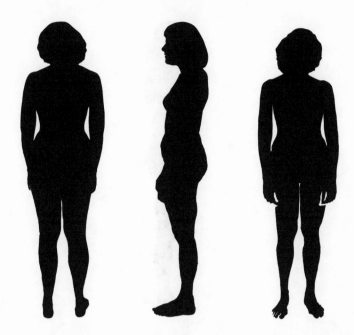

The reading begins in asking Jennifer to take a few deep breaths. As she does so, we subjectively gauge the degree of movement in the chest and the approximate percentage of potential breath she is actually mobilizing. We then ask Jennifer to breathe naturally, noting that she breathes shallowly, high in the chest, at about 60 percent of full capacity.

Beginning with a side view of Jennifer, we imagine a plumb line suspended from the ceiling of the room which intersects the middle of Jennifer's body. If Jennifer were ideally aligned with gravity, the line would intersect the middle of her ear, shoulder, hip, knee, and ankle. In Jennifer's case, we note that her head hangs forward of the line; her shoulders are slightly in back of the line; her hips are forward of it while her calves and ankles are behind the line. This is the common "reverse S" postural pattern noted by Ida Rolf, Moshe Feldenkrais, and other body educators — which results from a series of muscular compensations made by a body which is in constant conflict.

To understand these postural compensations, let's begin with Jennifer's head. The average adult head weighs approximately twelve to fifteen pounds. If the head sits squarely on the spine and shoulders, the gravitational pressure on the top of the head is equally distributed. If, as in Jennifer's case, the head is misaligned, compensatory tension is created in the muscles in back of the neck and upper back, which attempt to counter the force of gravity pulling Jennifer's head forward

and toward the ground. Whenever Jennifer is in the vertical plane, these muscles must tense and contract, in turn, creating opposing compensations in the shoulders, pulling them back in an attempt to equalize the tension.

The misalignment of the head, along with the compensatory mis-alignment of the shoulders and upper torso, cause the upper half of the body to sit forward of the pelvic basin, instead of sitting squarely in it. Gravitational pressure on the upper torso pushes it forward creating another compensatory tension-pattern in the sacrospinalis muscles, especially in the mid and lower back areas which must also remain chronically tense and contracted in opposing this forward pressure. Jennifer complained of lower back pain and occipital headaches.

Finally, in an attempt to compensate for the misalignments in the upper torso, Jennifer tilts her pelvis forward, locks her knees, and tightens her legs to counter and equalize the pressure on a torso pre-disposed to falling forward. The result is a body which, even at rest, is in a highly stressed condition and not at all comfortable.

From a front and back view of Jennifer, we observe that her right shoulder is higher than her left shoulder, and indeed, the entire right side of her appears to be pulled up.

Palpation of the muscles along the spine and lateral lines of the body reveals a higher overall tension on the right side of her body and chronically tensed legs which are cold to the touch.

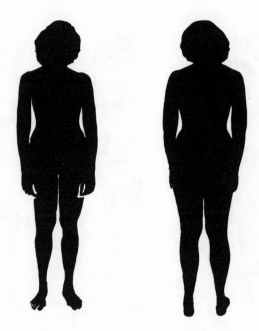

In noting the amount of open space between the lateral line of her torso and the inside of her arms, we observe that the higher tension level in the right side of her body is compensated for by cocking her head toward her left shoulder.

Jennifer supports herself almost entirely on her left leg and foot. Note that her right hand is higher than her left and that both arms are tensed — causing the hands to be brought forward of the thighs in a partial preparation response.

It is also noted that, as is usual, Jennifer's tipped pelvis is accompanied by locked knees and tense leg muscles which point her feet in slightly opposing directions.

A comparison of the upper and lower halves of Jennifer's body reveals a contracted, child-like chest area, with a contemporary, age-consonant lower body.

From this simple, physical reading, Jennifer appears moderately misaligned with her ground and reveals chronic tension in her legs and on the right side of her body, particularly in the neck and shoulders, lower back, and pelvis.

Psychological Profile

Observing Jennifer from a side view, once more, we observe that she obviously enters each life situation "head first" — not heart first,

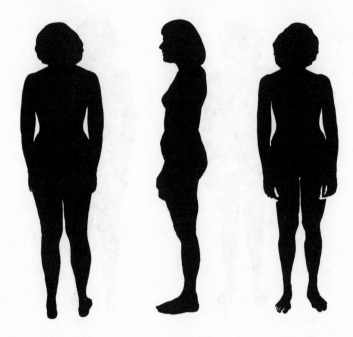

not belly first — not in an even and balanced way, but in a way which prepares her to scan, analyze and strategize each situation before she permits the rest of herself to engage the situation. She seems to move in from fear with wooden movement of her legs. She brings her head forward while she retracts her heart and genitals. She is used to doing this, but also appears uncomfortable doing so.

The observation that the left side of her body is more relaxed and grounded suggests that she may have been more comfortable functioning in the feeling/intuitional mode (i.e., left body is controlled by right brain hemisphere), but has forsaken it in favor of the perceptual/thinking mode of functioning.

Given that there is no genetic predisposition or history of skeletal trauma to account for these muscular tension-patterns, it would appear that Jennifer has learned to repress her emotions and sexual feelings by armoring the muscles in the heart area (e.g., neck, shoulders, chest) and by tilting her pelvis and tensing her legs and buttocks in an attempt at blocking potentially threatening sexual impulses emanating from these areas of her body.

Jennifer's tense arms and hands suggest chronic and suspended muscular preparation which may involve both defending herself from insults to her integrity, as well as reaching out to others for the contact,

support and nurturance she needs, but deeply fears, at the same time.

Her outward facing feet and toes, along with the unbalanced distribution of her weight suggests some misunderstanding and confusion regarding her motives, who she truly is, and where she is actually "heading."

If we imagine inhabiting Jennifer's body, for a moment, what might we experience? And, if we actually simulate some of Jennifer's muscular holding-patterns in our own bodies, much as subjects did in Nina Bull's research studies, what does this experience of lived-body tell us about Jennifer's interior world, and about her personal work toward conflict resolution and personal growth?

These physiological trackings of Jennifer's world might reveal that we are basically unsure of ourself, constantly obsessing on what is expected of us by others — followed by strategizing about how we might meet their expectations and gain their affection—always by appearing submissive and somewhat confused.

We might recall a time in our life when we were intuitive, and trusted our emotions to guide us and take care of us. Perhaps this bodily posture brings to memory the emotional pain and confusion which catalyzed our decision to block and numb our emotions and feelings in the first place—probably in an effort at psychological or physical survival. It might unfold a history of sexual trauma, rape or molestation, or a highly moralistic background where sexual exploration of any kind was forbidden under strict threats of punishment or abandonment.

Jennifer would later disclose that she was sexually molested and raped by her stepfather continually over a five year period, and that her mother, when informed of the abuse by Jennifer—at seven years of age —had denied the incidents, accusing Jennifer of making up "disgusting stories." Jennifer remained emotionally distant from her mother through to her death when Jennifer was sixteen years old. Her mother died of colitis. Recalling her mother's death brought tears to Jennifer's eyes, which she tried to cut off with her studied smile.

Therapeutic Profile

Jennifer's therapeutic goals, in her own words, were "to get through this depression and fear which I almost always feel and get on with my life."

Based on her body reading, it is suggested that Jennifer's therapy might involve learning to trust her feelings and emotions again by expressing the rage and terror experienced in connection with the sexual abuse perpetrated by her stepfather; finishing the grieving process connected with the loss of her mother, as well as her own ego-ideals; accepting her sexuality and her needs for contact, nurturance, and support from others; detaching from her conception of herself as a deficient and defective person while accepting and empowering herself as a person and a woman; and finally grounding her understanding of herself in a direct, assertive encounter with the here and now of her daily life, rather than obsessing over her concepts and fantasies of what those encounters "should be."

In summing up our body reading of Jennifer, it is helpful to note that our physical observations of Jennifer's posture are verifiable. When the head hangs forward of the shoulders, for instance, or when the torso hangs forward of the pelvic girdle, a chronic muscular holding pattern is created in opposing muscle groups in the neck and lower back, respectively. Body work, body awareness, and reeducation techniques, in releasing these tension patterns, lower the general stress baseline, producing a more relaxed posturing and greater body expressiveness.

In the psychological realm, our observations, though less objective and verifiable, do suggest some insights as to how Jennifer, historically and contemporaneously, relates to stressful events in her life.

But when we take these observations, insights, and hunches into the realm of the therapeutic, in terms of goals and processes, we must realize that we are, indeed, speculating, and that what is truly important in our body reading of Jennifer is only that which is meaningful to Jennifer. The psychotherapeutic encounter, if it is to be truly effective and meaningful, must begin from knowledge that we are uniquely different from one another and, ultimately, must discover who we are in realms far removed from our physical and psychological make-up.

Notes

1. Kurtz, Ron, and Hector Prestera, *The Body Reveals*, 1984, Harper & Row, New York, p. 106.

13

Body/Mind Healing

The inclusion of the body as a general source of knowledge to both client and therapist is changing traditional healing practices, first, by consolidating or expanding them into new ways of reading the body and contacting the client, and secondly, by blending into new ways of facilitating the client to contact and resolve his or her own conflicts of feeling, thought, perception, and action.

It would be impossible to, in any way, survey or illustrate the various combinations of psychotherapeutic techniques and approaches available to a therapist or counselor. The particular way in which a healer works surely rests on her or his own unique set of skills and sensibilities. And yet, the integration of bodywork and other forms of body/mind intervention, whether drawn from Bioenergetics, Behavioral Anesthesiology, Gestalt, Autogenic Training, Lomi Work, meditation, or an entire host of emerging approaches, is new to Western healing practices and deserves some attempt at illustration.

The vignettes, case profiles, and session notes which follow are drawn from the work of a dozen or so body/mind therapists, healers, and researchers. Like spying through the keyholes in some office doors, or overhearing a client's or therapist's account of the process, they are meant to communicate more of a flavor as to how body/mind healing proceeds.

Not all body/mind techniques, as you will see, necessarily involve touching the client, as much as bringing the individual's awareness to the experience of lived-body.

Let It Bleed/W. Banks

In this session, we are privy to the work of a therapist (T) facilitating a surgery patient (C) who continues to bleed, uncontrollably, following an acute gastrointestinal hemorrhage. Recognizing that the stress and confusion during these medical procedures are in themselves sufficient to induce a state of heightened sensitivity and sug-

gestibility, the therapist uses no formalized hypnotic/visualization instructions. During the angiography procedure, excess bleeding is
stopped, and later turned on again with the following instructions:

T: "This may seem strange to you, but has anyone asked you to stop
bleeding yet?"

C: The patient's quizzical look and verbal response of "no" elicited the
following short verbalization:

T: "Then why don't you stop bleeding? *NOW!* I know it *sounds* like an
unusual request, but it would really help us to help you; and after all,
you really have been controlling bleeding—all of your life—probably
without knowing consciously what you have been doing. You get cut or
scratched, and you *stop bleeding*, just like you increase your heart rate
when you get frightened, and you slow it down when you relax—you
do it but you don't know how. So you don't need to *consciously* know
how to stop your bleeding but it will help us if you just *let it happen
... now!*

At a later time, when it is required to turn the bleeding on again,
the therapist suggests the following:

T: "So far you have really done well. You have stopped your bleeding
completely. But in order to show what *was* bleeding, you now need to
undo whatever it was that you have done. You don't need to know how,
but just let it go ahead and bleed, *now,* so we can see if we have found
the correct spot." (Banks, W. Hypnotic Suggestion for the Control of
Bleeding in the Angiography Suite, 1985, *Ericksonian Monographs*, 1,
76–88.)

Puddle of Tears/Jim Doak

This session illustration involves Ann, a woman who has been in
therapy with Jim Doak for several years:
"She came into this particular session with no agenda, but
quickly noticed her chest was constricted when I asked her to focus on
her body sensation. Now, tightness in any part of the body is often an
attempt to say 'no' to something—no to letting something in (as when
a child tightens against a hypodermic needle) or no to something
emerging from within. Ann suspected that something was trying to
form internally and that she was fighting it.
"I asked her to tighten her chest even more and she said she felt
like a cement statue. I asked her about her life as a statue and she replied that she was strong, could be leaned on and had no feeling. When

asked what kind of feeling was best to be without she immediately replied 'hurt.' Now she and I knew what she was repressing, and as she came to this insight she began to cry softly. Asked to tell me all the people who hurt her, Ann listed them and her crying increased. Several times during her list she would begin to tighten against her feeling, twice beginning to get angry. I encouraged her to return to her hurt, not because anger is illegitimate, but because we were working with the softer gestalt of hurt and broken heartedness and I didn't want to interrupt one gestalt with another. Ann had much less difficulty with anger. She had always been an angry fighter, but it was her sustained softness and vulnerability that eluded her.

"As her hurt deepened and her tears came, she remembered her mother's sarcastic admonition, 'There you go crying again, you'll just become a puddle of tears.' I suggested she become just that, and she spread out on the floor, letting herself be the puddle her mother obstructed through humiliation. Her crying continued for a while as she let go of the chronic muscle tension in her back, the tension that kept her away from softer feeling but ready to fight. For now, she had given up fighting the tears that are an important part of living. For now she had a new way of experiencing her body ..." (Doak, James. *Coming to Life*, [1987, Blue Dolphin Press, Nevada City, California], pp. 127–128.)

Re-Parenting/Jack Painter

In this case profile, Jack Painter, a Reichian psychotherapist, profiles his first four sessions with a young, male client:

"Tony was an English 'skin head.' He considered himself tough and ready to confront authorities or rowdies who were not part of his gang. Underneath he was actually very needy. In the first sessions he wanted to express his anger as fully as possible. I supported this by provoking him with words and quick taps on the belly, but I waited for the moment he would accept more gentle work. During the fourth session after he had exploded with anger and was trembling in exhaustion, I rocked him softly and sang a lullaby. As he began sobbing, I was able, without much pressure, to begin moving previously resistant layers of tissue." (Painter, Jack W. *Deep Bodywork and Personal Development*, [1984, Mill Valley, California], p. 148.)

Face-to-Face Combat/Kate Walsh-Slagle

At the age of twenty-seven, Kate Walsh-Slagle was diagnosed as having multiple sclerosis, the "crippler of young adults." She profiles her work with me in a group session. Kate is now a psychotherapist in private practice in Nevada City, California.

"God, I'm scared. My mouth is so dry that I can barely get words out. There's Robert. He's the facilitator. I need to trust him. I have to hand my controls over to him. I will. He cares. That's what counts. I have to trust myself. I have to care enough about myself to trust me. No way to chicken out now. I'm out here in the center of a group of thirty people, requesting that I work first. That's so I won't have a chance to run out the door. I can't believe that I'm doing this, baring my soul. Bring on the demons, there's no turning back now. 'I don't want to die,' wails the woman who is on the floor. Who is making those awful, angry sounds? It's me! I never knew I could sound like this. Robert encourages me to stay with it. I trust him. I sense his gentleness and caring.

"My first confrontation is with the demon of multiple sclerosis. I'm in an altered state of consciousness right now, staring into the face of my fears about the disease. I'm visualizing having the disease. This is real, as my body cripples itself while I wrestle with the monster — the loss of control of my legs, arms and speech. Now I've lost my sight and I'm totally dependent, helpless, a vegetable. The fears seem to lose their powerful grip on me as I experience them in face-to-face combat. I've uncovered another demon — my own death.

"I take the suggestion, hesitating for a brief moment, to die — to experience my death. It is so dark and cold. I have no body, I'm floating. 'What is the worst part of dying?' questions Robert. 'Leaving all the people who are close to me — having to say goodbye,' I reply automatically. Now I'm saying goodbye to all the people I value. My heart is breaking. I'm really here. I'm sobbing, feeling incredible pain that I didn't know existed. Years of forgotten tears are rising up through my body and spilling out, as I hold, touch, and finish with each significant person in my life. I've lost all concept of time. The now moment of saying goodbye is all that exists. This now moment seems to last forever. There are so many people I love, so much to say to each of them, so very many tears.

"It's over now as I lie down again and reexperience my death. 'What is the worst part of being dead?' asks Robert gently. 'Being so very alone,' I respond. 'At what other time in your life have you felt this alone?' guides Robert. The corner of the kitchen, the coolness of the green wall, me seated on the beer case, shaking, crying — the image flashes through my consciousness. The insight dawns, illuminating my awareness. I've come full circle. Everything is so clear to me now.

"Grandpa isn't laughing. Horrible choking sounds are coming from Grandpa's throat. I'm on my feet. Ma is running from another room. Someone is shouting, 'He's dead, he's dead.' ... I run — escaping to the farthest corner in the kitchen. There's an old cardboard case where Pa keeps his beer bottles. Weak-kneed, I stumble onto it and resting my head on the cold green wall of the kitchen. I shake and cry ...

"Facing the demons about multiple sclerosis, my death, my grief at having to say goodbye, are only the beginning. My path is set in front of me. I'm feeling light. I'm feeling incredibly alive and excited ... It's all about movement. It's all about being alive!" (Slagle, Kate Walsh. *Live With Loss*, [1982, Prentice-Hall, New York], pp. 1 – 34.)

Golden Crumbs/Bernie Siegal

This vignette provides an account by a woman who started doing a combination of meditation and visualization during a recurrence of the breast cancer she had been treated for two years previously:

"I imagined small, delicate birds searching my breasts for crumbs. To my surprise, I imagined the cancer in the form of golden crumbs. Each day, the birds would eat these golden crumbs. After the birds had eaten their fill, I would then imagine a pure beam of intense, spiritual white light entering my body. I would then pray to God for guidance, renewal, and protection.

"One morning, after taking a bike ride, I sat down to do my meditation and visualization. The white light appeared immediately and coursed down through my head, spreading like white heat through my breasts and limbs. I felt the power take hold of me and I let go while my heart raced and pounded. After a short, intense interval, I slumped sideways in exhaustion. I knew something extraordinary had happened.

"The next morning, when I sat down to visualize, I could no longer find any golden crumbs. An inner voice whispered, 'There isn't anything there.' Each morning after that, I had the same experience."

A week later, according to Siegel, when this woman went in for a mammogram, all traces of her cancer were gone. (Siegel, Bernie. *Peace, Love and Healing*, [1989, Harper and Row Publishers, New York].)

Don't Leave Me/Don Johnson

The following vignette illustrates the work of Rolfing practitioner Don Johnson during a session with Ray:

"Ray is twenty years old, a chemistry major with his eyes set on a Ph.D. He rides horses, swims, runs every day. His first backpacking trip was when he was eight years old. His body is lean and athletic. For a month, he had been in constant pain and was about to withdraw from college. Visits to several specialists had been of no use. As a last resort, his doctor had sent him to be Rolfed. When I took his medical history, he reported only a slightly cracked ilium (the pelvic bone) the previous year, which 'had no effect anywhere else,' and that a horse had kicked him in the face. Other than that, he had been in top health, without accidents or diseases, until the previous month.

"If I were to have closed my eyes, I might have thought I was listening to a much older man, an accomplished intellectual with great social skills. He presented many pictures of who he was, 'I'm the kind of person who ... ,' 'I just can't see a thing,' 'I have an incredibly low pain tolerance.' His muscular system was like a web of taut piano wires.

"As we began to loosen the fascia of the pectoralis major ... allowing the breathing to flow more easily, tears came streaming out. They seemed unusually deep and filled with anguish. I commented that he seemed to have had years of painful experience. He replied, 'I have been in constant pain since the ninth grade.' I asked him what happened at that time. 'We were living in Morocco. My parents sent me away to school in Paris. I haven't lived at home since. When I was in Paris, I was hospitalized for a pain like the one I've been having lately. They couldn't figure out what it was.'" (Johnson, Don. *The Protean Body: A Rolfer's View of Human Flexibility*, [1977, Harper and Row, New York], p. 5.)

No Body Hears/Muriel Schiffman

In these session notes, Schiffman is facilitating the Gestalt approach of inner dialogue with Agnes — a young man who is dealing with conflicts surrounding physical abuse by her mother and abandonment by her father:

C: "I just don't feel like doing the work here. I don't feel like doing anything. I'm tired of always being so damned good. I want to quit my job and stop doing all the 'nice' things I've done all my life. I'm tired of being the perfect hostess ... I've never been this way before. I can't imagine what's come over me."

C: (as her *mother,* in a prissy, indignant voice.) "I can't imagine what's come over you. Why you *have* to be hospitable. That's the way we do things in our family. Now you behave yourself and do things properly ... That's enough!"

C: (Boldly) "Well, that's where I am now. I'm sick of doing things your way ... "

Mother: "Now that's enough of that. You'll just have to behave yourself. No more nonsense."

C: "I won't obey you anymore. I'm a big girl now. (Begins to tremble) I don't know why I'm shaking like this. I guess I'm scared ... "

Mother: (Fiercely) "How dare you talk that way! You think you can disobey me? I'll show you. I'll teach you! (Whips Agnes)"

C: (Crying) Oh, please don't! I'll be good. I want to be good, but I can never please you. Why do you spank me all the time, no matter what I do? Why should you want to hit a little girl?"

Mother: (Calmly hitting) "That's the only way to bring up a child. How would you know how to behave if I didn't spank you regularly? I have to do it."

C: "Somebody help me, save me! Daddy, please help me. Mother spanks me all the time and I'm so afraid of her. You don't know. You're not here when she does it. Please protect me."

Daddy: "I don't know what you mean Agnes. How can I help you? I have things to do. You'll have to excuse me now."

C: (Screams) "What kind of father are you? What kind of a man are you? Don't you give a damn about me? I'm your little girl and I'm so scared. (Agnes is still shaking. She lies down on the floor.) (Crying) I'm a little, little girl and I'm lying here on the living room floor crying, hoping someone will hear me and care. I'm so cold here in my nightie. Why won't anyone come and comfort me? Doesn't anyone care? Please, Daddy or Mother, come and put your hand on my cheek and tell me you love me. (Sobbing loudly) Just once tell me you love me. If I could just hear it once it would last me a long time. Nobody hears, nobody cares. It's so cold here. I'd better get up and go back to bed."

C: (As Big Agnes) "Get up Agnes, no point waiting for them. Just take care of yourself. Stop all that crying. It won't get you anywhere."

C: (As Little Agnes) "But I wish they would comfort me."

C: (As Big Agnes) "Well, they won't, so snap out of it."

C: "The shaking stopped. I don't feel scared anymore. Funny, I was so brave and rebellious. I didn't know I was scared underneath. I guess I have to change a little at a time, but I don't want to be her good little girl anymore. Boy, I'd like to shock her. (Laughs out loud) I know what I'd like to do! Go back to that small gossipy town and walk naked down Main Street. That would give my mother something to think about. She'd hang her head down for the rest of her life." (Schiffman, Muriel. *Gestalt Self-Therapy: Further Techniques for Personal Growth*, [1971, Self Therapy Press, Menlo Park, California], pp. 18 – 33.)

Touch Starvation/Julius Fast

In this vignette, Julius Fast offers us an illustration of how, being so intellectually oriented, we pay attention only to words, missing the messages a person is projecting with their hands, shoulders and eyes.

"Touching or fondling in itself can be a potent signal ... or a plea for understanding. Take the case of Aunt Grace. This old woman had become the center of a family discussion. Some of the family felt she would be better off in a pleasant and well-run nursing home nearby where she'd not only have people to take care of her but would also have plenty of companionship.

"The rest of the family felt that this was tantamount to putting Aunt Grace 'away.' She had a generous income and a lovely apartment, and she could still do very well for herself. Why shouldn't she live where she was, enjoying her independence and her freedom?

"Aunt Grace herself was no great help in the discussion. She sat in the middle of the family group, fondling her necklace and nodding, picking up a small alabaster paperweight and caressing it, running one hand along the velvet of the couch, then feeling the wooden carving.

'Whatever the family decided,' she said gently. 'I don't want to be a problem to anyone.'

"The family couldn't decide, and kept discussing the problem, while Aunt Grace kept fondling all the objects within reach.

"Until finally the family got the message. It was a pretty obvious message too. It was just a wonder no one had gotten it sooner. Aunt Grace had been a fondler ever since she had begun living alone. She touched and caressed everything within reach. All the family knew it, but it wasn't until that moment that, one by one, they all became aware of what her fondling was saying. She was telling them in body language, 'I am lonely. I am starved for companionship. Help me."

"Aunt Grace was taken to live with a niece and nephew ... " (Fast, Julius. *Body Language*, [1970, M. Evans & Co., New York], pp. 14 – 16.)

About Face/Jack Downing

The client is a highly educated woman of a wealthy Eastern family. A lovely, warm, wholesome looking woman, she has a slight twist to her smile caused by a scar which runs from the right side of her upper lip up along her nose. She has shared a recent dream with the therapist involving her conflicted feelings toward her overcontrolling, yet caring mother.

T: "Let's try an experiment. Now let's turn and look at each other. Now look in my eyes ... look in my left eye, OK? Now become aware of your face." (We are directly facing one another, each looking into the other's left eye.)

C: "My right side seems squished up. Like this." (She contracts her right facial muscles into a grimace.)

T: "Now, as we look at each other's eyes, consciously become aware of the tensions in your face and let go of them and relax." (Over a period of four or five minutes first her forehead loses deep furrows, then the cheeks and chin become soft. Finally the slight snarling tension of the nostrils goes, leaving only scar on the right upper lip.)

T: "Stay with the awareness of your face. And, as you find a tense area in your face, let your awareness go there. And just iron it out." (Pause.) " ... search out and let go ... put your awareness where you have scars." (Pause) " ... How does your face feel?"

C: "I feel ... (inaudible mumble) and I still have a skull fracture back here. And my facial scars are ... (inaudible)"

T: (applying hand pressure to the base of her neck.) " ... That's it, make some noise."

C: (First loud pants, then suddenly screams in terror over and over again, sobbing loudly.)

T: "Say, 'No!'"

C: "No! No! No! (Sobbing.)"

T: "Keep on saying, 'No! Mother!'"

C: "Mother ... mother, No! No! Mother! No! (Screams.) No! No! No! No! (Breaks down into loud sobbing.)

T: "Say it louder."

C: "I don't want it! I don't want it! ... No! ... No! No! No! No! No ... No!"

T: "Like this." (hits fist against the table.)

C: (hitting table with each "No!".) "No! No! I won't let you break me. I won't let you break me! I won't let you break me! No! (Slam, slam, slam, slam.) No! You ... No! (Pause.)

T: "Do you feel like going on, or do you want to stop here?"

C: (long pause.) "I'd like to go on, I'd like to finish her."

T: "I'm going to massage the base of your skull where you had the fracture; what was it, a car accident?"

C: "Yes, we were arguing and she didn't see a car coming from the left. I was thrown from the car."

T: "OK, I'll stop any time you say to stop." (Applies light and then increasing pressure behind her right ear ...)

C: "That hurts ... it's so sore."

T: "Let yourself go back to the accident, feel the accident."

C: "Damn you, damn you, damn you! You saw that car, you saw it. You will get your way if you have to kill me! (Pause; heavy breathing) ... I can't do any more." (Long pause.)

T: "How does your face feel now?"

C: "That's funny, now I feel the right side more clearly. There's still a dead spot here (touching her right cheek near the nostril) ... but the right and left sides feel almost the same."

T: "Check out your entire self, check out the whole right and left."

C: "Huh — right arm is still a bit stiffer, left feels nearly as strong. I'm more in balance, I'm almost entirely in balance."

T: "Let's stop here, OK?"

C: "Yes, I'd like to. Thank you ... " (Downing, Jack and Robert Marmorstein, eds. *Dreams and Nightmares: A Book of Gestalt Therapy Sessions*, [1973, Harper and Row, New York], 162–169.)

Holding Hands in the O.R./Henry L. Bennett

A tremendous gap exists between the use of surgical procedures in the operating room and established findings on the role of psychological factors, such as touch and caring, in facilitating the healing process in patients undergoing surgery. Henry Bennett offers the following case profile to illustrate how negative intervention can be replaced by positive intervention in the O.R.:

"A sixty-eight year old woman who had manifested evidence of heart disease but was unsymptomatic, was going to be operated on for a total hip replacement. In her preoperative examination, she had explained that during tense moments or when people argued, her heart felt like it swelled up and fluttered. After the anesthesia was administered, the surgeon entered the room, and as was usual for him, loudly expressed his displeasure at various aspects of the nurses' preparation of instruments. As the surgeon left to scrub, the electrocardiogram revealed a sudden decreased flow of blood to the heart, followed by sinus and then ventricular tachycardia (irregular heartbeats). Cardiopulmonary resuscitation (CPR) was applied, and the woman survived, having suffered a mild heart attack. The operation for the hip replacement was canceled, but there was no identification of reasons for the heart attack.

"The woman returned eight months later for the hip replacement, and the anesthesiologist, aware of her earlier experience in the operating room, sought to provide behavioral and psychological care. He visited the woman and in a twenty-minute conversation found her to be strong and perky, with a good wit. When he asked how she wanted to be treated during the surgery, she explained that surgery seemed to her to put a patient in a childlike position and that she therefore would like to be cared for as if she were a child. She asked to have her hand held and to be given encouragement and positive suggestions for her welfare. She also wanted soft music played into her ears during the surgery.

"These and other recommendations were followed on the morning of the operation. The surgeon came into the operating room just before the induction of anesthesia and went over to the patient's side. Until this point, the patient, whose hand was being held and who was quietly being offered words of encouragement, had been relaxed and calm. As the surgeon, whom she consciously liked and respected, spoke to her, she suddenly became nauseated and then vomited. The surgeon left the room to scrub, the nurses attended to the patient, who soon recovered her composure. Her recommendations were again followed, and she experienced a stress-free induction of anesthesia. On the surgeon's return, the anesthesiologist explained that the patient was extremely sensitive to conflict and might be the kind of person who somaticized easily. The anesthesiologist suggested that the surgeon refrain from loud argumentative behavior, that evidence of conflict might induce another, perhaps even more serious stress response. The surgeon behaved himself like a gentleman at a dinner party. The patient continued to receive good behavioral care throughout the surgery, and made such quick progress that the surgeon requested in writing that this type of service — behavioral anesthesia — be given to all his patients." (Bennett, Henry L. Behavioral Anesthesia, *Advances*, Institute for the Advancement of Health, Fall, 1985, 2 (4), 11 – 21.)

Open Faced/Richard Strozzi-Heckler

Richard Strozzi-Heckler, co-founder of the Lomi Approach, offers this vignette to illustrate how a body pattern can be connected to such an old memory that the individual may find herself reliving and being relieved of an area of repression and fear.

"M. B., a forty-five year old mother and advertising manager of a local newspaper, came to me complaining of chronic fatigue and a constriction in her breathing. Her health and domestic life were satisfactory, yet despite visits to various therapists and physicians she was plagued by a nagging chest tightness and vulnerability to chest colds. In my third session with her I worked in the area of her neck and upper chest. Her feelings of discomfort grew into fear and as I encouraged her into her feelings she became hysterical. She began to sob and her breathing became more and more constricted. As she began to resist and struggle with my hands I suggested she shout 'leave me alone.' When she did this a few times her face opened up and she took a full free breath. She suddenly remembered that as a child someone had held her down and tried to strangle her. She had completely blocked out the experience and despite many varied therapeutic experiences she had always suffered from tension in her neck and throat that resulted in a pinched voice. By facing the terror, fear, and anger of the experience that emerged during the bodywork she consciously integrated it into her being and received both a physical and emotional freedom. Her voice and body structure changed and she felt a renewed vigor and aliveness. The energy she had formerly used to repress that experience could now be used in a more constructive and conscious manner." (Heckler, Richard Strozzi, Lomi Body Work, *The Lomi Papers*, 1970, Tomales, California.)

Muscle Stretching/Carlson, Ventrella and Sturgis

Traditional relaxation training involves muscle tensing exercises to teach voluntary control of muscle tension, and the research shows varying results. In their research, Carlson, Ventrella and Sturgis use muscle stretching exercises instead of muscle tension exercises and report decreases in self-reported measures of anxiety, as well as reduction in muscle tension levels in their subjects. Their instructions involving the obicularis oculi muscles are presented below:

"Now, when I say 'begin,' I would like you to push up your eyebrows with your index fingers and push down your cheeks with your thumbs. Please note while you are stretching the muscles what the tension feels like and where the muscles are tense. Ready? 'Begin.' (Wait ten seconds.) Now quickly release the muscle tension, returning your hands to a resting position, and let the muscles around your eyes relax and become less tense. Continue to let the muscles relax until I tell you that we are ready to move on to the next muscle group. Tell the muscles to relax, relax (Wait sixty seconds)."

The muscle stretching procedure extended to left and right trapezius, left and right pectoralis, and left and right forearm/wrist flexor muscles. (Carlson, Charles R., Mark A. Ventrella, and Ellie T. Sturgis. Relaxation Training through Muscle Stretching Procedures: A Pilot Case, *Behavior Therapy and Experimental Psychiatry*, 1987, 18, 2, 121 – 126.)

Muscled Screams/John Pierrakos

In this description, John Pierrakos, a Bioenergetic Therapist, employs deep pressure on the jaw muscles to release the vocal component of repressed emotion.

"One way to handle these problems directly is to place the thumb of the right hand one inch below the angle of the jaw while the middle finger is placed at the corresponding position on the other side of the neck. The scalene and sternocleidomastoid muscles are grasped and pressure is applied steadily while the patient vocalizes at a high sustained pitch. The same process is repeated several times at the middle point and base of the neck, at different voice registers. Many times this leads to an agonizing screaming which develops into a deep sobbing and one can hear real emotional involvement and surrender. The sorrow is expressed in clonic movements and the whole body vibrates with emotion. The voice becomes alive and pulsating and the throat block is opened up. It is striking to discover what is hidden behind the facade of the stereotyped voice ... " (John C. Pierrakos, *The Voice and Feeling in Self-Expression*, [1969, Institute for Bioenergetic Analysis, New York], p. 11.)

Head Lock/Sigmund Freud

Although he publicly denounced touching of the patient in his
later writings, Freud employed touch early in his career in what he
termed the "concentration technique." Here he describes use of the
technique with a woman patient in treatment for hysteria:

"I decided to start from the assumption that my patients knew
everything that was of any pathogenic significance and that it was only
a question of obliging them to communicate it. Thus when I reached a
point at which after asking a patient some question such as 'How long
have you had this symptom?' or 'What was its origin?', I was met with
the answer, 'I really don't know.' I proceeded as follows: I placed my
hand on the patient's forehead or took her head between my hands and
said: 'You will think of it under the pressure of my hand. At the moment
at which I relax my pressure you will see something in front of you or
something will come into your head. Catch hold of it. It will be what
we are looking for. Well, what have you seen or what has occurred to
you?' (Breuer, J. and S. Freud. *Studies on Hysteria,* Quoted in C.
Monte, *Beneath the Mask: An Introduction to Theories of Personality,* [1987, Holt, Rinehart, and Winston, New York], p. 39.)

Jennifer Takes Heart/Robert Marrone

Jennifer, a twenty-nine year old woman, has been through twenty-
three sessions of body/mind psychotherapy (See previous chapter,
Body Reading.) Her nuclear conflict emerged in our sixth session when
deep body work on her leg muscles elicited the terror and rage connected to being molested by her step-father for five years, beginning at
the age of six. Her memories of the actual molestation were vague or
nonexistent until our thirteenth session — when acupressure applied
to her jaw muscles elicited vivid memories of being forced to perform
fellacio on her step-father.

In this session, Jennifer is immersed in the process of integrating
her life-long emotional distance from her mother with the memories of
being raped by her step-father.

She began the session with *reportage* about her childhood:
about the family's move from Minnesota to California when she was in
the fourth grade; the names of her two best friends in high school; and
the date of her mother's death when Jennifer was sixteen years old.
Whenever she mentioned her mother, I noticed that she held her breath
as she brought her hands to her abdominal area.

As she paused to gather her thoughts and memories, I asked her to close her eyes, then, to take a deep breath and to bring her awareness to the stomach area under the palms of her hands:

T: "Describe the sensations in your stomach, Jennifer."

C: "There's just a big knot."

T: "How big is the knot in your stomach?"

C: Oh, about as big as a tennis ball—and real hard." (Pressing her fingertips against her abdomen.)

T: "Give it a color, Jennifer, the first color that comes to mind."

C: "It's dark reddish brown—and disgusting."

T: "Take a deep breath now, Jennifer, and let your eyes remain closed. But allow your imagination to take over. Pretend that *you* are the reddish brown knot in Jennifer's stomach. Give the knot a voice—allow it to speak. Begin now, by verbalizing, 'I'm the knot in Jennifer's gut.'"

C: "I'm the knot in Jennifer's gut. I'm red and brown . . . and tough. And I just live here in Jennifer's gut, day in and day out."

T: 'What is your function, knot? What do you do in Jennifer's gut?"

C: "I keep her under control. (Long Pause) I make sure she doesn't get too pushy . . . doesn't tell any secrets to anyone. I make sure she's always a little scared—always a little frightened about everything she does, everyone she meets . . . otherwise, otherwise . . . she'd . . . she'd . . . (Jennifer's breath is caught in her throat.) She'd . . . "

T: "What would Jennifer do without you, knot—if you weren't there to keep her under control?"

C: (Jennifer began to tremble, her breath quickened and her eyes hardened as she fought to hold back her tears. She seemed to be shrinking into the chair when, suddenly, her posture changed as her body lengthened and her voice deepened into a ghoulish scowl.)

"She'd go crazy—just crazy. She'd go completely out of control. She's probably . . . ha! . . . not probably, she *would* begin crying and shaking. (Making fists.) And she'd get mad, really angry — and she might kill somebody—maybe her step-father—maybe herself. So, I keep her in tow—I have to."

T: "How long have you lived in Jennifer's gut, knot?"

C: "Since she was a little girl." (Jennifer remained motionless, then began to contract back into the chair, bringing her knees up toward her chest. With grimaced eyes, she spoke in the high-pitched voice of a young girl.)

"Since she was jus' a lit-el girl."

T: "Breathe, Jennifer. Keep your eyes closed and press your hands against the knot in your stomach — feel it — and now answer the knot, reply to it, you heard what it just said about controlling you — now tell it what you want to tell it."

C: (Sitting at the edge of her chair, sobbing, crying uncontrollably.) "I'm sick and tired of you. (Whispering) I'm not a little girl anymore."

T: "Louder."

C: "I'm not a little girl anymore — you can't treat me that way anymore."

T: "Say that again."

C: (Yelling) "You can't do that to me anymore." (Following a motionless pause, Jennifer slams herself against the back of the chair, slapping the sides of her limp hands against the arms of the chair.) "Where were you, mom? WHERE? Where were you? Where, mother, where ... ? Why couldn't I ever count on you?"

T: "Stay with your feelings now, Jennifer. Make your hands into fists."

C: "Leave me alone. You make me sick. You always make me sick — be quiet — I can't stomach you, go away, I can't stomach you." (Jennifer began to pound the arms of the chair with tight fists, repeating the phrase, "Where were you?", over and over again.) "That's what she would always say. (Rocking, sobbing) Whenever she was angry with me, she'd say that to me, 'I can't stomach you, I can't stomach you." (Sobbing)

T: (I pulled my chair next to Jennifer, asked if I could hold her and rocked her gently. She was curled into a fetal position.)

C: (Crying; soft voice) "When I went to her the first time, when I was about seven, I told her that daddy was doing 'bad things' to me. She kept demanding that I tell her all the details of where he touched me — how he did it — but all she'd say is, 'You're disgusting — you make me sick to my stomach with your filthy stories.' She never did a thing about it ... she never even tried to stop him."

T: (I held Jennifer until her crying had run its course. Moving my chair across from her, I watched as she patted her face with tissues.) "Want to take this one step further, Jennifer?"

C: "Yes."

T: "Go back to being Little Jennifer — that's right — shrink down into the chair again — that's it! Feel how small you are, how alone you are ... are you scared?"

C: (In small voice) "Yes, I am."

T: "Now, very slowly, begin to move — feel each muscle grow and expand as you get bigger and bigger. Breathe fully. Good, stay with it! Now, bring your feet slowly to the ground — and feel yourself get bigger and bigger as you slowly stand up. Breathe deeply." (Jennifer continues to rise from her chair.) "Bigger, get bigger — keep going." (Jennifer is smiling, hands stretched toward the ceiling.)

C: "Yes, yes!"

T: "That's it — reach for the ceiling — now slowly move your arms all around you — claim all the space all around you."

C: (Moving her arms, slowly dancing around the floor) "I don't need them anymore. (Laughing) I don't. I really don't."

T: "Now stand in front of your chair, that's it. Relax ... breathe — close your eyes. (Pause) Now, Jennifer, if you'll imagine the chair, you'll see a little girl huddled there. She's Little Jennifer. She's very frightened. Do you see her?"

C: "Yes, she's so small, so scared!"

T: "When you feel ready, bend down and pick her up and tell her what you want to tell her."

C: (Cradling Little Jennifer in her arms.) "You don't have to be afraid anymore — I've got you. I'll protect you. (Crying softly) I'll always protect you. Always. Always ... my sweet Little Jennifer."

T: "Now, as you inhale deeply, imagine that Little Jennifer enters into your heart — with each breath — find a place for her in your heart."

C: (With each breath, Jennifer's hands moved closer to her chest.) "I'll take care of you little girl, Jennifer will be here if you need her — we'll be OK now." (Jennifer sat quietly, hands on heart. After three or four minutes of soft crying, a small smile crossed her face.)

T: "What are you feeling now, Jennifer?"

J: (Sitting, with her hands still pressed against her heart) "I feel so complete (Pause) ... so much lighter ... at one with the world."

Part Four
Wonderwork

14

The Farther Reaches of an Embodied Psychology

> When one is interested in fear and not running from it, there is the possibility of a workable relationship with it ... Introduction into the institutional fabric of our society, from the elementary educational to the corporate business level, of such methods of learning as the martial arts, hatha yoga and body/mind oriented therapies, offers the possibility of truly reducing the suffering that results from fear and the reactions against fear. As a society, I hope we can learn about our fear before that fear leads to destruction.[1]
>
> — Robert Hall

Holism, although an abused, and often, confused term, simply refers to the theory that reality is composed of unified wholes that are greater than the simple sum of their parts — emphasizing the whole and the interdependence of its parts.[2]

Body/Mind Psychology, as an identifiable and dynamic force, has begun to give form and substance to a newer, more holistic body-of-knowledge. As this force of ideas grows and strengthens, it holds the potential to touch our lives in profoundly significant ways: from the ways in which we define our own individual personhood; to the ways in which we heal ourselves and others; to a planetary view of other species, nations and cultures as participants in a grand, global family.

Applying this theory to our own species, comes this definition from the Institute for the Study of Holistic Medicine: "Every human being is a holistic, interdependent relationship of body, emotions, mind and spirit ... (and) is best understood as this whole and dynamic relationship. The maintenance of continued good health depends on the harmony of the whole."[3]

Masculine Meets Feminine: Wholeness and Healing

Western concepts and approaches to healing have their centuries-old roots in a masculine point of view. Clinical psychologist Anne Langford[4] describes the masculine healing model along a number of in-

teresting dimensions: it concentrates on symptoms and parts and is in-
trusive; it deals exclusively with linear, cause-effect strategies; it views
disease states as problems, as "something wrong" or as alien enemies
to be destroyed (e.g., war on cancer, battle against AIDS, etc.); it uses
language which alienates and mystifies; it takes a professional stance
that the healer knows more about the healing process than the client;
practitioners take a strong, specialist approach; it focuses on vulnerability and death; and, it seeks a normative, empirical basis for understanding disease states while disregarding the unique make-up and circumstances of the individual patient.

As women exert a continuing influence on Western culture, especially in the healing professions, a complementary, feminine healing
model is reemerging.

The feminine healing model, according to Langford, is holistic in
nature and is reflected, not so much in new technologies and strategies,
as in shifting attitudes and values. This complementary model: recognizes diseases as an opportunity to learn and grow, and, at symptoms
as embodying messages that, when listened to, can be healing and en-
riching; it looks at the entire person and seeks to create a context or
environment where the healing process can unfold; its use of language
attempts to demystify the healing process; it recognizes and facilitates
the patient's responsibility (i.e., ability to respond) in the healing process; it focuses on life and accepts surprise, movement, and flux as part
of the process; and, it is an open system which places great value on
compassion, loving care and the uniqueness of the person.

The masculine model, based on the theory of classical physics,
has, and continues, to serve us in profound and powerful ways in cur-
ing, as well as managing, numerous human diseases and disorders.
And yet, with recent breakthroughs in psychoneuroimmunology, body/
mind psychotherapies and health psychology, we can, perhaps, more
than simply wonder about the possibilities opening to us as these
once separate models, masculine and feminine, intertwine and merge
into one.

Consider some recent research conducted by Boston University
psychologist David McClelland[5]: When college students viewed a film
of Mother Teresa, Nobel Peace Prize laureate, tending to the sick and
dying in the slums of Calcutta, their immune functioning, as measured
in concentrations of epinephrine and immunoglobin, increased immediately — even in students who had previously reported that they dis-
liked Mother Teresa. "The results," McClelland suggests, "means that
she was contacting these consciously disapproving people in a part of
their brains that they were unaware of and that was still responding to
the strength of her tender loving care."

One can only marvel at the educational, medical, and spiritual implications of this and related research findings which suggest that engaging in or observing another person engaged in the heartfelt act of loving and caring for others may have important functions for the health of the individual and the community as well.

From the perspective of Body/Mind Psychology, the central point is that the masculine model, by itself, is constrained from asking "unscientific" questions, such as, what is the role of loving and caring in the healing process? Likewise, the feminine model, while likely to assert that loving and caring do enhance the healing process, is, by itself, constrained from fully verifying the assertion without applying scientific strategies and technologies. Joining the two together, however, as a unified, holistic paradigm, removes all the old constraints and begins to suggest new and powerful insights into the processes of healing, communication, and conscious living.

Pain Meets Joy: Wholeness and Personhood

In schizophysiology, as we have seen, our three brains work in continual conflict — each attempting to overpower the others. We live each day shifting from one to the other in some chaotic cerebral dance. Often, the result is physical disease, emotional breakdown and confusion of thought.

However, we also know that certain states of consciousness — certain moments — have the potential to change our compartmentalized brains into integrated, healthy brains. Suddenly, a previously nonexistent form of intercellular conversation takes over — our multiple brains become one — and we experience full embodiment, and, in turn, new modes of perceiving, feeling, thinking, and moving.

Psychologist Abraham Maslow, founder of Humanistic Psychology, was one of the first to make clear that a complete and holistic understanding of personhood must include, not only the study of pathological conditions, but, equally, the study of healthy, creative, life-nurturing conditions. His work prompted the creation of a psychological force to complement the classical psychoanalytic viewpoint, which tends to ignore our positive, loving, cooperative nature. "To simplify the matter somewhat," he stated, "it is as if Freud supplied to us the sick half of psychology and we must now fill it out with the healthy half."

Maslow's theory of personhood involves the development of what he called "self-actualization," which he defined as "the full use of talents, capacities, potentialities." Like incomplete gestalts, Maslow viewed these capacities and potentialities as a chorus waiting to be heard. "Capacities," he said, "clamor to be used, and cease their clamor only when they are used sufficiently."[6]

In focusing on the healthy half of psychology, Maslow succeeded in balancing human pain and suffering with the joy and triumph of human love, creativity, and courage. He termed these fulfilling, high-toned moments "peak experiences ... a generalization for the best moments of the human being, for the happiest moments of life, for experiences of ecstasy, rapture, bliss, of the greatest joy."

"All peak experiences," he continued, "may be fruitfully understood as completions-of-the-act ... as the Gestalt psychologist's closure, or the paradigm of the Reichian type of orgasm, or a total discharge, catharsis, culmination, climax, consummation, emptying, or finishing."[7]

Maslow's studies of self-actualizing individuals involved extensive analyses of living persons, as well as historical figures, who would, by popular definition, be seen as creative, mature, fulfilled, and so on. Supported by numerous research studies by others over the years, Maslow compiled a list of traits that he believed were characteristic of self-actualizing people:[8]

1. They have a more efficient perception of reality and are better able to accept uncertainty and ambiguity in others.
2. They tend to take others for what they are and are not guilty or defensive about themselves.
3. They are more spontaneous in their thinking, though their everyday actions and appearance may be quite conventional.
4. They have what they consider to be important goals and are more concerned with problems than with themselves.
5. They prize their privacy and do not mind being alone.
6. They are able to be independent of their environment.
7. They reveal a continued freshness of appreciation for repeated experiences.
8. They report mystical experiences, oceanic feelings, and feelings of wonder, awe, oneness, and loss of self.
9. They have social interests and a feeling of connectedness with all of humanity.
10. They have deep, close relationships with a few well-chosen individuals.
11. They have a democratic character structure and are relatively indifferent to birth, race, color, sexual orientation, religion or gender in judging other people.

12. They tend to enjoy activities for their own sake, but also appreciate the difference between means and goals.
13. Their sense of humor tends to be philosophical rather than hostile.
14. Their creativity, which might be in any field of endeavor, often involves the generation of fresh ideas.
15. While not rebellious, they tend to be generally independent of any particular culture.

Of course, as Maslow made clear, the self-actualizing process does not mean an end to problems, difficulties, pain, and suffering in the individual's life. Such an individual does, however, tend to initiate challenge and excitement by seeking new situations in order to utilize the "clamoring capacities." This thrust toward personal expansion and growth makes the probability of peak experience not only more possible, but more fruitful, in that they will tend towards completion of personal experiences rather than remain partially fulfilled.

For Maslow, the self-actualizing process and the increasing ability to achieve peak experiences were the core of a new psychological mode in which we seek to develop a relationship with the transcendent, the spiritual; for each of us to discover that we are part of a bigger and grander *gestalt*. In this sense, he called for an embodied psychology which speaks to the transpersonal, the transhuman and the transworldly experiences within us. He said, "We need something 'bigger than we are to be awed by, and to commit ourselves to it in a new, naturalistic, empirical, non-churchly sense, perhaps as Thoreau and Whitman, William James and John Dewey did."

Maslow made the spiritual quest the centerpiece of his psychology of personhood. "Without the transcendent and the transpersonal," he said, "we get sick ... " And yet, modern Western culture, all in all, has resisted this view of the transpersonal and spiritual — branding it as unsuitable for scientific investigation. Maslow stated, " ... it is almost impossible to speak of the 'spiritual' life (a distasteful phrase to a scientist, and especially a psychologist) without using the vocabulary of traditional religion. There just isn't any satisfactory language yet."[9] Consequently, the notions of "transcendence" or "spirituality," in the world of the psychologist smacks of the occult, the mystical, the out of touch. For this reason, traditional psychologists have shied away from investigation of it as from a hot stove. Instead, they have been more comfortable with the sick, the diseased, and the disturbed — focusing their energy on the logos of suffering and pain. The results of

their investigations prove, without a doubt, that human beings are suffering animals. Yet, there is a neglect of the opposite position, that human beings are bounding transcenders, creators, and healers—and it
is this position which also needs to be examined—and with the same
investment as has been given to the study of pain and suffering.

Abraham Maslow refused to pay homage to a psychology which
he viewed as half-hearted and incomplete. And, in seeking a middle
ground, where pain melded with joy, and suffering with triumph, he
was one of a very few who pointed the way to an embodied, holistic
psychology.

East Meets West: Wholeness and Global Community

Today, as interest in a holistic point-of-view continues to grow,
Western thinkers are more apt to view the concepts and philosophies
of Eastern cultures as fruitful fields of study. In this regard, we must
pay tribute to Psychiatrist Carl Jung as, perhaps, the first major thinker
to bridge the gap between Eastern and Western bodies-of-knowledge.
A magnificent scholar and investigator, Jung called for a synthesis of
Eastern and Western concepts in order to better understand our psychological life as individual beings and as beings interconnected in a
grander global community.

Committed to a middle ground, Jung avoided the devaluation of
Western modes of thought, as well as the overvaluation of Eastern
modes. Rather, he called for an integration of the two. He said, "Filling
the conscious mind with ideal conceptions is a characteristic feature
of Western theosophy ... One does not become enlightened by imag-
ining figures of light, but by making the darkness conscious." And further, "It seems quite true that the East is at the bottom of the spiritual
changes we are passing through today. Only this East is not a Tibetan
monastery full of mahatmas, but, in a sense, lies with us."[10]

Yet, there was contradiction in all of this attempt at synthesizing
East and West—even to Carl Jung.

In the West, we view human integrity in terms of strengthening
the individual sense-of-self via increased autonomy, self-esteem, and
personal independence.

The major focus of Eastern models, however, is on the ingrained
tendency for each individual to become more closely attuned to the
Brahma—to a sense of an undifferentiated something greater than the
individual self.

We arrive, therefore, at two formerly distinct cultural viewpoints
on the psychology of humankind: one centered on the Differentiated,

on personal growth and individual autonomy; the other centered on transpersonal growth and the tendency to expand the boundaries of self so as to merge with the Undifferentiated. And yet, in Jung's estimation, it is in the marriage of these two points of view, in their merging and blending, that a fuller and deeper understanding of the human experience might unfold.

Psychology Meets the Tao: Wholeness and Embodiment

Today, as growing interest in a global, holistic approach unfolds, it is becoming practically a truism to say that we are all part of a larger system: that the life of the bacteria is connected to the life of the insects, and to the world of plants, in turn to the world of humans, and so on. We now know that just as the interconnectedness of parts makes up the whole, so the whole is but another part of a still greater whole.

But, what may be self-evident today was not so yesterday. In decades past, the forties, fifties, and into the sixties, there existed a sort of compartmentalized, social isolation. We struggled together — in body and/or spirit — against the barbaric Hitler; we lived in idyllic little towns and bustling cities, with Beaver/Cleaver families, with defined goals, roles, holes — with God very much on our side. Much of it provided the appearance of interconnectedness and harmony. However, it was, for the most part, *illusion*.

The truth, as we would discover in retrospect, was that the illusion was built on factors which isolated us from each other: black from white, blue collar from white collar, male experience from female experience, normal from abnormal — on and on — all so clearly defined and well-founded, or so we thought.

These segregating factors came into view more clearly as we learned that pesticides killed not only the bad bugs, but also the good ones — and the white crane in the blue water — and everything else connected to the living world; or as racism lit fire to the cities; or as blue-collar workers demanded a larger piece of the apple pie; or as the all-American family splintered in the aftershock of centuries of inequality between women and men; or as God abandoned the United States in Viet Nam; or as valium, cocaine, and alcohol spread through the bustling cities and then into the suburbs and rural townships as self-medication for dealing with the overwhelming isolation. And then into the late seventies and eighties, cloaked in an attitude that came to be called narcissistic — the "me" decades — that were centered on self-image, profit, greed, and which, eventually, found many of us awash in samsara.

Today, it seems quite evident that, as one songwriter put it, " ... castles made of sand fall to the sea, eventually." But not then, except by a few whose vision, intuition, and common sense, could grasp the destructiveness of fragmenting factors that were destined to alienate us from each other; to make prisons of our bodies and psychic traps of our minds.

Contemporary psychology can no longer deny that every society ever studied, every anthropological unit ever observed, relates to some universal force perceived to be bigger than any individual member, and grander than the society itself. Twentieth century physics and neuroscience have opened a door into the world of the transpersonal and spiritual in the form of the hologram. More and more, those aspects of human brain function which fit the mathematics of the hologram help account for those human experiences which, up until now, have remained outside our grasp. The possibility appears strong that as further discoveries unfold, a rapproachment between what have been divergent, if not hostiley, conflicting views of human nature, will take place.

From the perspective of a Body/Mind Psychology, a psychology of personal and transpersonal healing must begin with the lived-body — and the embodied experience of being related to a factor greater than the individual ego.

As the conflict between divergent views of human nature is replaced with complementarity of differing views, Body/Mind Psychology promises newer approaches to psychotherapy which are more efficient, economical, powerful, and longer-lasting than traditional, exclusively verbal approaches. In creating these more integrative forms of healing, education, and communication, we are relying increasingly on a Taoistic point of view where, like body/mind, formerly inseparable opposites converge and blend into a more complete understanding of the psychological process and human functioning.

Body/Mind Psychology is asking each of us to recognize that the increasing fragmentation of society — with its split-level perspective that allows love and compassion to co-exist as neighbors with violence and atrocity without seeing itself as split — results, fundamentally, from the schism between body, mind, and spirit which we have inherited. And that the separation of wholes into fragments, and then into mere slivers, right down to tiny atoms, gives birth to both the beneficial light by which we see, as well as the hideously blinding light by which we shall see no more.

The longer we remain disembodied and depersonalized, the greater our loss of empathy with each other — then the more likely we are to objectify each other as individuals, groups, and nations. And the longer we remain disembodied, the more likely we are to sink deeper into delusion and deception — all the more reason to become more aware of the lived-body—to take it seriously, as a constant "truth" the mind can never be.

The more we deny and delude ourselves and each other, through our narcissistic games and strategies, the more we harden our eyes and restrict our vision, the more our bodies react in kind, with restrictions, blockages, stresses, and diseases.

A soft body, on the other hand, a body aware of itself, creates an embodied experience of self and other which facilitates the mind to relax and broaden its split and restricted vision. To put it another way: an armored body creates an armored mind creates an armored society — overreactive, rigid, militaristic, ecologically destructive, and less and less able to create for itself a healthy, positive world vision—but, rather, confines itself to creating mind-sets that allows for the gradual destruction of its own global habitat, and the personhood of its own inhabitants, to be greeted with little more than a shrug of its collective shoulders.

The more embodied we are as individual beings, the more we may heal ourselves as a community. It is an ancient and profound concept, but one increasingly lost to lip service. As the Roman philosopher Juvenal articulated it, *mens sana in corpore sano* — a sound mind in a sound body meant a healthy, strong, and vital society.

Wilhelm Reich argued that body and mind are unitary — two sides of the same coin—but no model or paradigm existed at the time to allow for the full development of such a perspective. During the forty years or so, since his major works were published, the same questions have arisen over and over again: how can body and mind be one and the same?; how can a mental event, a desire, a feeling, an intention be the same as a discharge of neurons or a muscular patterning at some zone of the body?

Today, our knowledge of physiological psychology and neuroscience has made clear how certain body structures are intimately involved in organizing the sequence of movements we call emotions, perceptions, and thoughts; and how these events are aroused in each of us. Our knowledge of clinical psychology has taught us that emotions, perceptions, and thoughts may be disguised, and how each influences the other in sometimes subtle, and at other times, in overpowering and devastating ways. All of these aspects speak to the same reality, but, like the story of the blind men and the elephant, each interpretation emphasizes only one or another important piece of the puzzle; objective-subjective, external-internal, body-mind, and so on.

Wilhelm Reich believed that our body-of-knowledge, and its underlying assumption that separates body from mind, was the cause of mental distortions, physical diseases and the loss of emotional empathy between human beings — and the authorities called him "crazy." And now, little more than a quarter century following his death, in a world held hostage to Uzi terrorism, nuclear contamination, and chemical pollution; in a world of everyday poverty, violence, heartlessness, and loss of meaning, we may begin to see how very prescient Reich was. And, more importantly, we may begin to speculate on how Body/Mind Psychology might promote a healing process to bind the wounds within us and between us.

A bridge to our understanding is under construction — a synthesis of major proportions is unfolding, and with it, a new force is emerging in contemporary psychology. Like a butterfly on the wing, it is unlike anything that came before it because it is not merely a new approach — or a new theory — but a fundamental restructuring and revisioning of the limits we have, for centuries, placed on knowledge itself.

As we shift to this new paradigm, it becomes clear that theories, research, and practices which explore and promote body/mind unity have profound and immediate implications in psychotherapy, communication, education, child-rearing, medicine, and in the training of physicians, nurses, teachers, and other caring professionals. No human service, of whatever kind, can be more than temporarily effective that does not take into account the whole person — the mind, the body, and the spirit as an integral unit.

Today, as we prepare for entry into the new millennia, Body/Mind Psychology is a beginning attempt to ask the most burning of questions, and it is this: how do we make use of this new body-of-knowledge before we bring about our own destruction? And there is, of course, no simple answer or solution. But there may well be a small, but highly significant first step we might each take in arriving at a solution — based on a profound insight embodied in Body/Mind Psychology, namely, that *awareness, in and of itself, is curative.*

Notes

1. Hall, Robert. Fear, Violence and the Body Experience (with Thomas Pope and Ron Boyer), *Lomi Papers*, Summer, 1980, p. 7.

2. Smuts, Jan Christian. *Holism and Evolution*, 1961, Viking Press, New York.

3. Pelletier, Kenneth. *Holistic Medicine: From Stress to Optimum Health*, 1979, Delacorte Press, New York.

4. Langford, Anne. The Feminine Approach in Healing, *The Laughing Man*, 1984, 5 (1), 48–52.

5. Ornstein, Robert and David Sobel. The Healing Brain, *Psychology Today*, March, 1987. 48–52.

6. Maslow, Abraham. *Toward A Psychology of Being*, 1968, Van Nostrand, New York, p. 5.

7. ————. *The Farther Reaches of Human Nature*, 1971, Viking Press, New York, p. 105.

8. See n. 6 above.

9. See n. 6 above.

10. Jung, Carl. *The Collected Works of Carl Jung*, Bolinger Series XX, Princeton University Press, Princeton, New Jersey, p. 265–66.

Suggested Readings

de Chardin, Teilhard. *The Divine Milieu*, 1960, Harper and Row, New York.

Corsini, Raymond J. and Danny Wedding. *Current Psychotherapies: Fourth Edition*, 1989, F. E. Peacock, Itasca, Illinois.

Cousins, N. *The Healing Heart*, 1983, Norton, New York.

Ehrenreich, Barbara. *Fear of Falling: The Inner Life of the Middle Class*, 1989, Pantheon, New York.

Elkins, David N. et al. Toward A Humanistic-Phenomenological Spirituality: Definition, Description and Measurement, *Journal of Humanistic Psychology*, 1988, 28 (4), 5–18.

Goleman, Daniel and Richard J. Davidson. *Consciousness: Brain, States of Awareness and Mysticism*, 1979, Harper and Row, New York.

Grof, S. *The Adventure of Self-Discovery*, 1988, SUNY Press, Albany, New York.

Hayward, Jeremy W. *Shifting Worlds, Changing Minds: Where the Sciences and Buddhism Meet*, 1989, New Science Library/Shambhala, Boston.

Kane, M.D., Jeff, editor. *Healing: A Physician/Patient Communication Journal*, The Health Communication Research Institute, Sacramento, California.

Jung, Carl. *Man and His Symbols*, 1964, Doubleday, New York.

Krishnamurti, J. *Life Ahead,* 1963, Quest Books, Wheaton, Illinois.

Locke, Steven and Douglas Colligan. *The Healer Within: The New Medicine of Mind and Body,* 1986, New American Library, New York.

Lyons, Joseph. *Experience: An Introduction to a Personal Psychology,* 1973, Harper and Row, New York.

Maslow, Abraham. *Toward a Psychology of Being,* 1968, Van Nostrand, New York.

Maslow, Abraham. *Religions, Values, and Peak-Experiences,* 1970, Viking Press, New York.

Neumann, Erich. *Depth Psychology and a New Ethic,* 1973, Harper, New York.

Ornstein, Robert and David Sobel. *Healthy Pleasures,* 1989, Addison-Wesley, New York.

Peck, M. Scott. *The Road Less Traveled: A New Psychology of Love, Traditional Values and Spiritual Growth,* 1978, Simon and Shuster, New York.

Pelletier, Kenneth. *Holistic Medicine,* 1979, Delacorte Press, New York.

Prescott, James. Body Pleasure and the Origins of Violence, *The Futurist,* April, 1975.

ReVision: A Journal of Consciousness and Change, Cambridge, Massachusetts.

Reynolds, David K. *Flowing Bridges, Quiet Waters,* 1988, SUNY Press, Albany, New York.

Sayama, I. *Samadhi,* 1986, SUNY Press, Albany, New York.

Schmookler, Andrew Bard. *Out of Weakness: Healing the Wounds That Drive Us to War,* 1989, Bantam Books, New York.

Tageson, C. William. *Humanistic Psychology: A Synthesis,* 1982, Dorsey Press, Homewood, Illinois.

Trungpa, Chogyam. *Journal Without Goal: The Tantric Wisdom of the Buddha,* 1981, Prajna Press, Boulder, Colorado.

Tulku, Tarthang. *Knowledge of Freedom: Time to Change,* 1984, Dharma Publishing, Berkeley.

Watts, Alan. *The Wisdom of Insecurity,* 1951, Pantheon Books, New York.

Watts, Alan. *Psychotherapy East and West,* 1961, Ballantine, New York.

Index